Not Too Awful Bad

A Storyteller's Guide to Vermont

Also from Islandport Press

down the road a piece: A Storyteller's Guide to Maine by John McDonald
Live Free and Eat Pie: A Storyteller's Guide to New Hampshire by Rebecca Rule

My Life in the Maine Woods by Annette Jackson
Where Cool Waters Flow by Randy Spencer
Stealing History by William D. Andrews
Shoutin' into the Fog by Thomas Hanna
Nine Mile Bridge by Helen Hamlin
The Cat at Night and *Hardscrabble Harvest* by Dahlov Ipcar
The Scallop Christmas by Jane Freeberg and Astrid Sheckels
A is for Acadia by Richard Johnson and Ruth Gortner Grierson

These and other great books are available at:
www.islandportpress.com

Not Too Awful Bad

A Storyteller's Guide to Vermont

by Leon Thompson

ISLANDPORT PRESS

ISLANDPORT PRESS • YARMOUTH • FRENCHBORO

Islandport Press
P.O. Box 10
Yarmouth, Maine 04096
books@islandportpress.com

www.islandportpress.com

ISBN: 978-1-934031-27-8
Library of Congress Control Number: 2009936447

First edition published October 2009

Book design by Michelle Lunt / Islandport Press
Cover Design by Karen Hoots / Hoots Design
Front cover photo mural by the Open Doors After
    School Program, featured on the Peoples Trust
    Company building, St. Albans City, Vermont
Illustrations by Leslie Mansmann

Dedication

To the Park Café, in St. Albans, Vermont—
the best home office on Earth.

To Kurt Singer—
I wish you could read this one.

To my friend Lee J. Kahrs—
you're next.

To Julie—
the June to my Johnny.

Thanks . . .

Credit goes where it's due. And I'll start first and foremost with whoever invented the Internet. Nice work. Makes my job easier.

Also, thanks to Mimmo's Restaurant and the Cosmic Café & Bakery, in St. Albans City, for letting me monopolize space and Wi-Fi while I worked, and when the Park Café wasn't open. A monstrous shout-out also goes to tech god Patrick Warn, who opened his closet and made me mobile.

More importantly, I owe something—maybe gift cards—to my cache of personal sources and storytellers, hereafter known as "The Crap Pack": Slim Bovat, Mom, Dad, Bebo, MeMe Laroche, PePe Laroche, Grandma and Grandpa Thompson, Uncle Turk, Suzy, Marcie, Kristy, Dianna Baraby, Clarice, Wendy V., Jessi, Kathy, Champ, Pauline, Marybeth, Jennifer, Michelle, Jenn, Warren Kimble, Jim Fisk, Phyllis Potter, the Newton brothers, Sara Jane Luneau, Dan, Nut, Butch, Eric, Clifton, Fran, the naked tour guide at Maple Glen Inc., Peter, Larry, Howard, Dicky Boy, Gerald Barney, Wendy M., Mingo,

Tony, Chuck, Liz, Emily, Aunt Ruthie, Eli, Sara, and my friend and author-in-waiting, Hannah Taylor, for this icebreaking Vermont story:

Seems Hannah was working at a local convenience store when her buddy Ben Montagne came in with his friend, Nate. Ben cashed out with his debit card, while Nate stood next to him. Hannah asked for Ben's PIN. Ben started to punch it in. Then he stopped and looked at Nate. They grinned over the numbers: 9530.

"Biggest John Deere you can thinka," Ben said.

Take air.

Table of Contents

Yee-ellow! I'm Leon Thompson

Frankly? I am not the most qualified Vermonter to write a guidebook about Vermont. That would have been the late Slim Bovat.

Slim's native Vermont life would fill a trilogy of books and likely begin with his legendary claim that he started "chewin' tabacka" when he was six years old. Hard to believe, considering that, back in his day, Vermont students couldn't even bring their cigarettes to school until they were at least seven. (Eight, in more progressive counties.)

Slim was one of those Green Mountain octogenarians who resisted such useless, nonsensical trends as "computers," or "iPods," or "running water," yet he wasn't too proud to break down and sign a cell phone contract. It was a Vermonty way of saying, "I know more than ya think."

Slim swore by his cell phone, but, initially, he had a problem with it: his hands. Decades of dairy farming had turned Slim's hands into baseball gloves with four hot dogs and a Twinkie attached to each. Hands like that make it hard for a man to store a credit-card-sized cell phone in his Dickies shirt pocket and answer calls quickly—before they go to voice mail.

Slim was missing calls. Slim hated missing calls. So Slim fixed it.

He found a piece of sturdy string and duct tape. (Almost a fact: Vermont law requires duct tape in every household.) With the tape, Slim attached one end of the string to his cell phone and fastened the other end to a pen. A good, thick pen. Not one of those thin, blue, plastic pens where the ink freezes while you're milking in January.

From then on, when Slim's cell phone rang, he yanked the pen from his Dickies shirt pocket, fished out his cell phone, and answered.

"Yee-ellow!" (That's how Vermonters answer cell phones. "Yee-ellow!" It's a bona fide Vermont greeting. More on that later...)

Just when Slim thought he had his cell phone all figured out, another obstacle arose. His oversized fingers kept interfering with those tiny volume control buttons, so the person on the other end either got **TOO DAMN LOUD**, or Slim couldn't make out a word they were saying.

So Slim fixed it.

He got his duct tape. (He didn't have to look far.) Then he found a matchstick. He yanked his pen from his Dickies pocket, fished out his cell phone, and stuck the matchstick to the tiny volume control buttons. From then on, when Slim had to adjust his cell phone volume, he simply pressed either end of the matchstick. He never started a fire. Far as I know.

"It's quite a get-up," said his granddaughter, Lisa.

Slim's cell phone was very Vermont. Slim was very Vermont. That's because, as I said, Slim was a native Vermonter.

I'm not Slim, but I, too, am a native Vermonter.

I was born in St. Albans (pronounced "Snobbins," if you're native) and raised eight miles north, in a small riverside town called "Swah'in" (pronounced "Swanton," if you're non-native). Swanton is home, no matter where home is.

Mom was one of ten children; Dad was one of eight. My maternal grandparents' ancestors crossed into Vermont from Canada, which explains the strange pronunciation of my first name—"Le-IN," not "Le-ON." Actually, another Le-IN grew up in Swanton, and another in Fairfield, a nearby farming town. Le-IN: It's a French-Canadian thing.

My grandmothers were strong, smart homemakers. While PePe Laroche—Mom's father—worked on his 500-acre dairy farm, Grandpa Thompson served the railroad. His long hours of exposure to loud train engines sparked hearing loss and yet another mispronunciation of my name: "Le-urn." (He can't hear how he says it. Poor guy.)

Lots of my relatives hunt, fish, and cruise through mud bogs atop four-wheelers (ATVs, or all-terrain vehicles, for you city folks). I don't, although I enjoyed fishing as a child, especially during those rare moments I didn't catch weeds or—this really happened—tree limbs.

Usually, they were behind me.

I couldn't cast well.

I was what you'd call an "inside kid." I started reading *Mad* magazine when I was in fourth grade. While the other kids were in their backyards, I was in our living room, playing along to ABBA eight-tracks on the piano we didn't have—namely, our couch—or developing my uncanny impersonations of The Fonz ("Ayyy!"), W. C. Fields, and Pee-Wee Herman.

"You weren't wrapped too tight," says Uncle Turk, Dad's youngest brother. "You still aren't."

True.

If I can be nakedly and brutally honest here—and I'm a Vermonter, so I'm allowed—I never believed Vermont fit me, and vice versa. I felt like a tea bag in a fishbowl. I always sought an escape, right from childhood. Vermont is a small state, and I thought I was bigger. At age eight, I walked into our kitchen and told Mom my dream of being a famous comedian. She laughed. To me, that was a start.

My high school guidance counselors asked me: "What do you want to be after high school?"

"Gone," I'd say.

I was George Bailey with braces.

Unfortunately, colleges and universities do not offer "comedian" as a major. Also, schools cost money. Lots. So I spent four years at Lyndon State College, a small liberal arts school in Vermont's gorgeous Northeast Kingdom.

At Lyndon, I majored in radio and then English, and started writing a humor column for the college newspaper, *The Critic*. My column was called "Pronounced Le-in." (I made that up all by myself. Clever, eh? Just wait until I get going here.)

My first two books, *Good Junk* and *dork: another look at my junk* are collections of (mostly) humor columns I've written in thirteen years of journalism. I enjoy telling stories. Other people's. And mine—as long as other people relate to my stories. Otherwise, it's all just blah, blah, blah.

The book you are holding contains stories and jokes from all sides of Vermont, from all kinds of people connected to it. Some of these jokes and stories are mine. Some aren't. You'll know the difference. If not, just ask. I'm here to help.

You're probably wondering if I ever grew an affinity for Vermont. Sure did. I lived and wrote in South Carolina for two-plus years. As you might discern, South Carolina is not Vermont. I enjoyed South Carolina and learned a lot there, especially on that day the state literally shut down after a two-inch snowfall, which, to me, was like taking a shower—normal. But frightening. I have never been so scared to drive in the snow. Not because of the snow, but because of the inexperienced southerners that drove in it with me. (In South Carolina, highway workers cover roads with beach sand during snowfalls. No. Joke.)

When I returned to Vermont in 2000, I realized it is not merely New Hampshire turned upside down. (Find a map. It's freaky.) My advice to Vermont's inside kids is to leave. "Go," I say. "And come back. Rediscover the unique, magnificent, bucolic state that you so foolishly resented for so long. Trust me, you'll be a better Vermonter for it."

I hope I am.

The famous promotional slogan says, "I (heart) VT."

Me? I dig Vermont.

I dig that when I wake on a midsummer morning, and it looks like a John Denver song outside my open windows, I have several options: run by the lake, bike on the recreation trail converted from a dormant railroad bed, or spend the day at a local nudists' campground. (True story. You'll see.)

I dig that I come from the first state to abolish slavery and the first state to tell people, "We recognize the love you have for someone else, no matter who that someone else is." I dig wondering what will happen next in this tiny state that regularly shifts the world's large eyes on it.

I dig Vermont Teddy Bears and Ben & Jerry's and the fact that all my out-of-state friends ask to see Church Street in Burlington just minutes after they get off the plane.

I dig living in a town so small that people often say, "Hey, there's the guy from the newspaper," but large enough where others could give a damn who I am. Pockets of anonymity do exist here, no matter what you hear.

I dig that so many of my music-loving friends will ask, "Have you ever met any of the guys from Phish?"

Yup. Mike Gordon. The bassist. I dig his hair.

I dig that I've also honed a pretty dead-on impersonation of Vermont's independent U.S. senator, Bernie Sanders. I'll do it for you, if you ask. Nicely.

You don't want to hear my Howard Dean. It's loud.

When she was six, my daughter, affectionately known to me as "Bebo," invented her first recipe: Smash Mash. It's one part tilapia, one part brown rice, one part corn, and one part cottage cheese, all mixed together in a bowl.

I dig that Vermont is a big bowl of Smash Mash.

So, I suppose I'm qualified to write this book because I am a native Vermonter who digs Vermont. Plain. And. Simple. We all know there are tons of books about Vermont on shelves and in libraries—from historic texts and outdoor guides to photo collections and novels that make Oprah cry—but not many native Vermonters wrote those books.

But, again, I'm probably not the most qualified native Vermonter who could pen a book about Vermont. That would be Slim Bovat, and other Vermonters like him.

Keep in mind: This book is a guide aimed at helping you comprehend the thicker and finer points of this state. Also keep in mind: I'm only one Vermonter. Go easy on me. I haven't

seen or done everything, so, inevitably, I'll miss something—
maybe a few somethings. I don't ski. (Many natives don't.) I
don't own a single piece of camouflage clothing. And I've never
tipped a cow, only because any cow that's waited on me hasn't
deserved a tip.

Cows stink at keeping your coffee hot.

Slim Bovat
March 22, 1923–May 19, 2009
May Heaven have plenty of duct tape.

1

Some Vermont Basics

Getting Here

Vermont is easy to find. We're small—the forty-fifth-largest state in the nation—thanks to a good nutritionist and trainer.

Vermont's greatest width is at the Canadian border: 89 miles. The narrowest width is 37 miles, at the Massachusetts line. From north to south, Vermont is 159 miles long. Its belly button is the town of Washington.

Vermont's land area is 9,250 square miles, about the size of Denver. Our population hovers around 600,000 people, and, on average, our visitors make an estimated 14 million trips annually and spend about $1.5 billion on goods and services, making tourism our top industry.

Vermont's Green Mountain range forms a north-south backbone that runs most of the length of the state, slightly left of center—where many Vermonters lean politically, too. About 77 percent of Vermont is covered by forest; the rest contains meadow, uplands, lakes, ponds, and swampy wetlands. Vermont is 98 percent white—and I don't mean when the snow flies.

Residents of British ancestry live throughout most of Vermont, but the northern part of the state has a high percentage of people with French-Canadian ancestry. Beginning in the 1980s, the Burlington area welcomed resettlement of several refugee communities from Southeast Asia, Bosnia, Somalia, Burundi, and Tibet. (We do tend to mix it up a bit now and then.)

By car, the major route into Vermont is Interstate 91, which enters southeastern Vermont at Brattleboro, about three and a half hours from New York City, or seven and a half hours from Washington, D.C.

Another main route is Interstate 90, also known as the Massachusetts Turnpike (or, as many Vermonters call it, "Masshole Highway"). From there, you can connect to Interstate 91 at Springfield and head to Brattleboro (about ninety minutes). Or, take a more scenic corridor: up U.S. Route 7 in western Massachusetts to Bennington (about an hour, and Route 7 runs a straight, easy pattern up the length of western Vermont, too).

From eastern Massachusetts and southern New Hampshire, you can drive up Interstate 93 to Interstate 89 and enter the state at White River Junction.

A recommendation: If you are in Brattleboro and want to eventually reach northwestern Vermont—and if you're not rushed—cross to Bennington on U.S. Route 9 West, through the southern Green Mountains, and then connect to Route 7 North. Route 9 is known as the Molly Stark Trail, named for the wife of a New Hampshire general who became a hero in the Battle of Bennington, during the Revolutionary War. Be careful with Molly Stark, though, especially in winter, when snow drifts onto the road. She's slick.

While researching this book, I drove Molly Stark's winding, wintry roads with my father's 2003 Mustang convertible, which he let me use for the road trip. Just before Bennington, while descending a sharp, curvy slope, I saw a pickup truck heading east and upward, pulling a red snowmobile on a trailer.

Without warning, the snowmobile flew off the trailer and into the guardrail. Ker-smash! (The driver wasn't hurt. Just mad.)

"Welp," I thought, "there's no weight on the trailer now, which means it can only go one way."

It got so close I could read the registration letters on its side. And just as I pictured my father's head in his hands, sobbing at the sight of his totaled Mustang, the trailer snapped back and let me continue on my way.

See how much I dig Vermont? I almost died while writing this book.

You should buy another copy.

Vermont's northern neighbor is Canada. Contrary to popular belief, Vermont is not in Canada and never seceded to Canada. We considered it, though.

From Montreal, the best way to reach Vermont is by Autoroutes 10 and 35 to Route 133, which connects to Interstate 89 at the border. There are several ports of entry

Speaking of treacherous roads, now would be a good time to pose a sincere, serious question to all you flatlanders who think it's fun to speed up and down the winding Smugglers' Notch Road. Here's the question: What the HELL are you THINKING?!?!
"What?" you ask. "I just wanna do some rock climbing and hiking. There are good spots along the road for that." Yes, I know. But do you NOT realize this eight-mile stretch of white-knuckle-worthy road in Stowe has more blind spots than a Braille novel? Would you play chicken on a roller coaster?
I didn't think so.
Here. Stay home and watch this instead:
www.youtube.com/watch?v=uLuDhJ4HrUM

A beautiful, sunny Saturday in March. Snow melting. Sap running. For Vermont, in March, it ain't getting much better.

My friend Kathy and her two grandchildren are invited to a Fairfield sugarhouse for the afternoon. They pack a lunch and wait for Margaret, whose family owns the sugarhouse, so they can follow her. It's now one-thirty in the afternoon. No Margaret. They call Margaret's number and her husband, John, answers the phone.

"Yee-ellow! . . . Yut . . . Yut . . . Welp, she left about an hour ago . . ." John gives Kathy directions to the sugarhouse: Go to Fairfield and take the second left-hand turn past the school that burned down. Easy enough.

Kathy takes that left-hand turn and starts up the road. No need for a steering wheel. This time of year, the mud maneuvers your car along the ruts for you.

No sugarhouse. Anywhere. Kathy stops at a house, knocks on the door, and gets new directions from the kind man who answers: "Go to the end of this road, make a left, and then turn on the second dirt road on the left."

So they do. And they're still wrong. They try several more roads that are covered in melting snow and mud soup. Restless, frustrated, and defeated, they decide nonetheless to try one more place for directions.

The man at the next farmhouse says, "Oh, sure, that's easy. Just go to the school that burned and make a left-hand turn on the second dirt road."

"Talk about coming full circle," Kathy recalled. "We did eventually find the right sugarhouse. What everyone forgot to tell us is that the school that burned had been repaired and turned into housing."

into Vermont across the state's northern border, from Highgate Springs (in the west) to Derby Line (in the east).

If you decide while visiting Vermont that you'd like to pop up to Canada, take caution: Once you enter Canada, you might not reenter the U.S again. Ever. This is called "Homeland Security."

Way before the rules tightened, we native Vermonters who lived in border towns visited Canada regularly to:

1. see relatives we hardly knew
2. eat Chinese food
3. get sloshed (the drinking age in Canada is eighteen).

Sometimes, we'd combine numbers two and three. In Franklin County, where I grew up, there are no less than 40,000 Chinese restaurants to accommodate 40,000 residents—a staggering ratio. Nonetheless, when we wanted Chinese food in the 1980s and 1990s, we went to the most logical place we knew: Canada. We'd raid their buffet tables and then their bars, though not always in that order.

But I digress. If you do decide to visit Canada while you're here, I hope you can get back. If not, I'm sure you'll learn to love Celine Dion and hockey.

Getting around in Vermont

Although Vermont is easy to get to, it's not necessarily all that easy to get around in, once you're here, especially if, like most tourists, you're not sure where you're going. For cripes' sake, I've lived here most of my life, and I still don't know the difference between Marshfield and Waitsfield.

When traveling through Vermont, the directions you receive often include obscure and esoteric landmarks, such as an old church, a convenience store, or—most popular—someone's farm or house or both.

"Yut. I can git ya air. You just go two miles down this road, take a left, take another left, take your third right, go past the Longway farm about a half-mile, and it's right off your next left, past the Larose house."

There is one major benefit to driving in Vermont: No toll roads. Anywhere.

As if everyone knows the Longways. Or the Laroses.

Transportation options

Cars are not always the safest mode of transportation in Vermont. Come to think of it, neither are the roads. A Vermonter once got arrested and charged with felony driving under the influence after police found him drunk on his riding lawn mower. His blood-alcohol level was .16—twice the state's legal limit of .08—but a jury acquitted him, even with three prior DUI arrests on his record, because the lawn mower fit the definition of a tractor under state law, not a motor vehicle.

With that in mind, you might want to research these other transportation options in Vermont:

Burlington International Airport: 1200 Airport Drive, South Burlington, 802-863-1889, www.btv.aero

Amtrak: 800-872-7245, www.amtrak.com

Greyhound Bus Lines: 800-231-2222, www.greyhound.com

New England Vacation Tours: 802-464-2076, www.sover.net/~nevt

Vermont Bicycle Touring: 802-453-4811, www.vbt.com

Lake Champlain Transportation: for information on ferries that cross Lake Champlain into New York, 802-864-9804, www.ferries.com

Vermont Public Transportation Association: www.vpta.net

Vermont

★ **State Capitals**
◉ County Seat
● Cities 100,000-499,999
● Cities 50,000-99,999
· Cities 10,000-49,999
· Cities 0-9,999

— ·· International Boundaries
— — State Boundaries
—·· — County Boundaries

——— Toll Roads and Bridges
——— Interstate Highways
——— U.S. Highways
——— State Roads

········· Major Rivers
——— Intermediate Rivers
⌀ Lakes

The regions

Essentially, Vermont is split into five main regions:

Southern Green Mountains: Vermont's green and white license plates are a minority here, especially during foliage and ski seasons. Tourists love the Southern Green Mountains area, which includes Brattleboro, Bennington, Manchester, and the Okemo Valley.

Route 4: U.S. Route 4 cuts across Vermont, from White River Junction to Rutland—with Killington, Quechee, and Woodstock sandwiched in between—and features some of the state's more popular attractions, including Quechee Gorge, the Vermont Institute of Natural Science, Billings Farm & Museum, Killington Resort, and the New England Maple Museum.

The Northern Green Mountains: This area features Montpelier, the nation's smallest state capital, and the only Ben & Jerry's factory in the state that offers tours and free samples (in Waterbury). Mad River Glen ski area is here, along with the Vermont Historical Society Museum, and the city of Barre, which has been dubbed "The Granite Capital of the World." Yabba. Dabba. Doo.

The Northeast Kingdom: The NEK is in a world of its own, and it's a great world. This is where I went to college (Lyndon State) and discovered some of my favorite places on Earth: Lake Willoughby, the Fairbanks Museum and Planetarium, Cabot Creamery, the Kingdom Trails Network, and Bread & Puppet Theater.

The clincher, though, is Joe's Pond in Danville. If humans could have two hearts, Joe's Pond would fill my second one— all of it. Joe's Pond has a magnificent general store, a quaint campground on the water (Point Comfort), and one of the state's more popular events: The Joe's Pond Ice-Out, which was a result of some serious cabin fever during the 1980s.

Annually, thousands of people nationwide—and some from overseas—buy tickets and wait for a cinder block that sits on the ice to drop to the pond floor; this means "the ice has gone out." The ticket-holder who has the date and time closest to the ice-out wins a big pot o' money. (Want to play? Go to www. joespondvermont.com/iceout.html.)

The Champlain Valley: Home. It's where I grew up. It's where I live (as of this paragraph, anyway). Burlington is here—the smallest, largest city of any state—and it's home to the University of Vermont and Champlain College. Also, to The Flynn Theatre, Missisquoi National Wildlife Refuge, St. Albans' Taylor Park, Enosburg Opera House, the Chester A. Arthur Historical Site in Fairfield, the Shelburne Museum, the Vermont Teddy Bear Company. There's so much . . . so, so much.

West of northern Champlain Valley is the Lake Champlain Islands region—or Grand Isle County—which includes North Hero, South Hero, and Alburgh. In October, South Hero hosts the annual Applefest, which might be the best apple festival in New England (802-262-5226). This region also contains St. Anne's Shrine, a gorgeous Catholic pilgrimage site (www.saint annesshrine.org).

Lake Champlain

In his 2009 book, *Don't Go There: The Travel Detective's Essential Guide to the Must-Miss Places of the World*, Peter Greenberg, travel editor of NBC's *Today* show, lists Lake Champlain as a "must-miss water location."

Lake Champlain "has been polluted with an abundance of phosphorus for the past thirty years, and it's only getting worse in several parts of the lake," Greenberg wrote, blaming urban development for phosphorus-heavy runoff. "The water often looks cloudy and green and smells foul, due to algae blooms, and the depletion of the lake's oxygen has affected fish."

I won't lie. Peter Greenberg is right, but he embellishes. Lake Champlain is not a cesspool, and state and local efforts are under way to clean it, though it will take time—lots of it.

Vermont is the only New England state with no coastline along the Atlantic Ocean, and Lake Champlain makes up about 50 percent of the state's western border, although parts of Lake Champlain are also in upstate New York and Quebec.

Lake Champlain is the sixth-largest body of freshwater in the U.S.: about 435 square miles in area, 110 miles long, and 12 miles across at its widest point. Its maximum depth is approximately 400 feet. The lake varies seasonally from about 95 to 100 feet above sea level, and it does rise above flood stage, mostly during spring thaw, and depending on how many fishermen pee over the sides of their boats in any given year.

Lake Champlain briefly became the nation's sixth Great Lake on March 6, 1998, when President Clinton signed Senate Bill 927, which reauthorized the National Sea Grant Program. The bill contained a line that declared Lake Champlain a Great Lake, a status that would have allowed Vermont and neighboring states to obtain federal research funds. The Great Lake status was rescinded on March 24, following a small uproar, and after President Clinton learned Champ was an unattainable male.

Ah, yes—Champ. Our own Loch Ness monster. Some authorities write off Champ as mere legend, but others believe he lives deep in the lake and is possibly a relative of the plesiosaur, an extinct group of aquatic reptile. Others have tried to achieve Champ's fame—Memphre, Champ's purported cousin in Lake Memphremagog; the Lake Willoughby monster in the Northeast Kingdom; a giant water serpent in Brattleboro—but there is only one Champ.

To date, there have been more than 300 Champ sightings, and not all during our famous Grateful Dead shows of the 1990s. Champ sightings go back as far as the late 1800s, and passengers on the steamboat SS *Ticonderoga* claimed they saw a lake creature in 1945. Nine years later, someone trapped a fourteen-inch reptile (Champ's baby?) in Shelburne Bay.

 Last year, I caught up with Champ at St. Albans Bay, where, like me, he was enjoying his first spring-thaw cigar on a warm, late-April night. During this exclusive interview, The Scaled One finally spoke out on his upbringing, his love life, and what he's doing to help clean the lake he calls home.

Sheriff Nathan H. Mooney claims he first saw you in 1883, from fifty yards away, where he stood on shore. That was fifty years before the Loch Ness controversy. Just when did you come to be?

I dunno, me. I do know that my father, H. B., was a Texas oilman who saw a better future in dairy farmin'—not a bright dinosaur, really—so he came to Enosburg. My mother, Kris, moved to Montgomery from Long Island. They met at a Halloween party.

Is it true about you and Nessie?

We were so in love. (*He pauses and gazes out at the water.*) She was beautiful—long, long neck. Great teeth. Huge humps. Dragon breath. But when my popularity caught on in Vermont, the Scots decided they needed Nessie to boost their tourism industry. Being a legend was her dream, so I encouraged her to leave, thinkin' she might return, if it was meant to be. I haven't heard from her since. (He sniffles . . .)

Do you think there's another chance for you two?

This is Vermont. There's always another chance for everythin'.

Well said. Talk to me about P. T. Barnum.

That jerk never met a dollar he didn't like. He offered $50,000 to the person that would bring him my carcass, so that he could put me in his World's Fair show. Thinking back, I should have sent him a fake one, like an oversized sturgeon or something. He never wootuv known.

Has anyone really ever seen you?

Oh, sure. The real Vermonters. They don't yank out their video cameras or try to shoot dozens of pictures of me with hopes of gettin' on TV or in the paper. We chat about the weather, fishin', politics. It's an unspoken agreement: I don't eat them, and they don't tell.

Is Lake Champlain as dirty as some say?

It depends on the messenger, at this point, not the message. The government says it's doin' a lot—to promote its agenda. The environmentalists say the government isn't doin' enough—to promote their agenda. This lake is like anything else: perfectly imperfect. It's here. It's home. I've survived in it this long. This lake ain't goin' nowhere.

What do you do to keep it clean?

I never bathe my cows in the water—unlike some people.

What's the one thing you want people to understand about you that they probably don't?

I like my privacy, really.

Then why did you agree to this interview?

I didn't, Leon. You said you'd pay me fifty bucks and get me a twelve-pack of Bud if I put on this Champ costume and read the parts that you wrote in this . . .

Click . . .

Okaaayyy, well . . . uh . . . it appears my . . . um . . . my recorder's battery died at that point in the interview. Yeah. That's what happened. But special thanks to Champ for emerging from seclusion and speaking to the world.

Ahem . . .

In 1977, Sandra Mansi, a Connecticut flatlander, took the most famous photograph of what she called a "dinosaur" in Lake Champlain, and, in 1995, Dennis Hall of Champ Quest—a group dedicated to the aquatic enigma—claimed he recorded Champ on video. With Pamela Anderson.

Champ is a huge draw. Port Henry, N.Y., has erected a giant model of Champ and holds "Champ Day" on the first Saturday each August. Champ is also the mascot of Vermont's lone Minor League Baseball team, the Vermont Lake Monsters (formerly the Vermont Expos), who play their summer season at Centennial Field in Burlington.

The Peter Greenburgs of the world would have us believe we market Champ heavily to distract tourists from Lake Champlain's pollution issues, but Champ predates Peter Greenburg and all his brouhaha. The original Iroquois and Abenaki tribes that lived near Lake Champlain had legends about a sea creature called "Tatoskok," which, when translated, means "future baseball mascot."

Lake Champlain contains several bays, and Vermont has numerous other water bodies, including: the Brewster River, Connecticut River, Lamoille River, Missisquoi River, Ottaquechee River, Trout River, Winooski River and the West River; Joe's Pond in Danville, Lake Dunmore in Salisbury, Lake Willoughby in the Northeast Kingdom, Lake Morey in Fairlee, Lake Carmi in Franklin, and the Wrightsville Reservoir in Montpelier. Not to mention all our cricks.

There are probably more. I just haven't fallen in them yet.

2

Vermont History

Let's start with a (sometimes accurate) Vermont timeline (with some help from the Vermont Division for Historic Preservation):

8500– Glacial activity creates the Champlain Sea; Paleo-
7000 BC Indians explore and hunt in Vermont; voters elect Democratic attorney Patrick Leahy to the U.S. Senate. He eventually becomes the state's longest-serving senator.

7000– Archaic Period; native tribes move seasonally
1000 BC around Vermont to live, hunt, gather, fish, and campaign for Leahy's reelection.

1000 BC– Woodland Period; native tribes establish villages
1600 AD and develop trade networks, along with ceramic and archery technology. A developer applies for a permit to build the state's first Wal-Mart under Act 250, the state's controversial and (oft-perceived) cumbersome land-use law. The store opens in 1996.

1535 French explorer Jacques Cartier is the first European to see Vermont. He spends the weekend skiing.

1609 Samuel de Champlain discovers Lake Champlain by peeing in it from the side of his ship.

1666 Fort St. Anne is constructed on Isle La Motte, which is French for "cheap, Catholic souvenirs."

1690   A small British fort is built at Chimney Point, now an unincorporated community in Addison County. In 1749, Swedish explorer Pehr Kalm visited Chimney Point and wrote, "I found quite a settlement, a stone wind-mill and fort in one, with five or six small cannon mounted; the whole enclosed by embankments. Within the enclosure was a neat church, and through the settlement well-cultivated gardens, with some good fruit . . . apples, plums, and currants. But, sadly, no Chunky Monkey or Chocolate Chip Cookie Dough."

1724   The British build Fort Dum at Dummerston, quickly add a 600-square-foot expansion, and change its name to Fort Dummer.

1731   The French build a fort and begin settlement at Chimney Point. Still no Chunky Monkey. *Merde!*

1770   The Green Mountain Boys organize to protect New Hampshire land grants offered by corrupt New Hampshire governor Benning Wentworth. The mobilization spawns other militia groups, including the Green Mountain Girls, the Green Mountain Cross Dressers, and the Green Mountain Freaks Who Post Weird Photos of Themselves on Craigslist.

1774   The Scottish-American Land Company brings Scottish settlers to Ryegate and Barnet. No one understands a frickin' word they say.

1775   Ethan Allen makes Fort Ticonderoga one of his Facebook friends and then captures it.

1776   While America swiftly prepares for the coke-and-disco-fueled bicentennial celebration 200 years later, Mount Independence is constructed in Orwell.

1777 Vermont declares itself a republic in Windsor and adopts an inaugural constitution that outlines male suffrage, public schools, and the abolishment of slavery (a first in the nation).

The Battle of Bennington?

On August 16, 1777, an American victory occurred during the Revolutionary War when 2,000 New Hampshire and Massachusetts militiamen, with help from the Green Mountain Boys, defeated 1,250 enemy soldiers. To this day, August 16 is celebrated as a legal holiday in Vermont—Bennington Battle Day—and a 306-foot tall monument in Bennington commemorates the fight. Only it happened in Walloomsac, New York, ten miles away. Really.

1779 Vermont establishes property rights for women.

1787 Castleton, Vermont's first college, is established and chartered by the Vermont General Assembly. The next year, Castleton forms its first fraternity: Phi Kappa Cowpie.

1791 Vermont becomes the fourteenth state in the U.S.; the University of Vermont is chartered and soon becomes known as "Groovy You-vee;" Thomas Jefferson and James Madison visit the state, which now has 85,341 people, 85,000 of whom come from somewhere else, i.e., they're transplants. (More on them later.)

1801 George Perkins Marsh, America's first conservationist, is born in Woodstock; Brigham Young is born in Whitingham. Young would later leave to lead the

Mormons from Illinois to Utah, because he thought Vermonters drank too much Magic Hat.

1805   Montpelier becomes Vermont's capital and quickly earns the nickname "Montpeculiar."

1829   Chester A. Arthur, the twenty-first president of the United States, is born in Fairfield. Well, maybe. While most official references list Fairfield as Arthur's birthplace, centuries-long speculation has persisted that Arthur was born in Ireland, or Canada, and that he was unconstitutionally the twenty-first U.S. president. That would make him the only U.S. president to disregard the U.S. Constitution, right?

1855   A Republican becomes Vermont governor, a trend that would last until 1962, much to the chagrin of Pat Leahy, who, by this time, has outlived Santa, the Tooth Fairy, and the Easter Bunny combined.

1864   The St. Albans Raid, the northernmost action of the Civil War, occurs on October 19 when Bennett H. Young and his bumbling band of Confederate idiots steal $208,000 from local banks and fail to burn the town after their four-ounce bottles of Greek fire won't work.

(Get this: They were never punished.)

1872   Calvin Coolidge, America's thirtieth president—and, along with Ronald Reagan, Herbert Hoover, and Woodrow Wilson, one of the few prezes with an alliterative name—is born on the Fourth of July in Plymouth Notch.

Three newly married Vermonters were sitting together, bragging about how they had given certain duties to their brides. The first man married a woman from Alabama.

"I told her she was gon' do all the dishes and keep that house clean," he boasted. "It took a couple days, but on the third day, when I got home, all the dishes were washed up and put away."

The second man married a woman from Florida.

"I ordered her to do all the cookin', cleanin', and dishes," he crowed. "The first day, I didn't get any results. The next day was better. By the third day, the house was spotless, the dishes were done, and I had a huge steak dinner on the table when I got home from work."

The third man married a Vermont girl.

"Welp," he began, "I told her she had to clean the house, wash the dishes, mow the lawn, do the laundry, and make a hot meal three times a day."

Intrigued, the other two men leaned in and listened.

"On the first day, I didn't see anything. On the second day, I didn't see anything. But by the third day, most of the swelling had gone down in my left eye, so I could see enough to make a sandwich, load the dishwasher, and call a landscaper."

1918   Women vote in town elections. Men keep their mouths shut after they hear about that other guy's left eye (see box).

1919   Poet Robert Frost moves to Vermont and inspires a movement for hundreds of Vermont poets who sadly discover that when everyone starts taking a road not taken, it's not so not taken anymore.

1922   Centennial Field is constructed at UVM's ballpark in Burlington. Rumors quickly spread about the field's use of steroids.

1930	Cows officially outnumber people in Vermont, which makes for some pretty interesting senior proms.
1950	The Marlboro Music Festival is established; 377,747 people live in the state; Pulitzer Prize winner Pearl Buck, a Virginia native, moves to Winhall.
1953	The SS *Ticonderoga* makes its last steamboat trip on Lake Champlain and eventually finds a permanent home with the Shelburne Museum.
1964	Victory, Granby, and Jamaica become the last towns in Vermont to receive electricity—and just in time to see The Fab Four on *Ed Sullivan*. Whew!
1968	Billboards are banned in Vermont. Some people believe marijuana is, too.
1994, 1995	The Grateful Dead play two consecutive summer concerts at the Franklin County State Airport, in Highgate; 60,000 people attend the July 1994 show; 100,000 people attend the June 1995 performance, possibly because of the opener: Bob Dylan.

Ummm . . . this is a bit embarrassing, but . . . umm . . . anything after those Grateful Dead shows is reeeaaallly foggy for me. I know that, somewhere after that, Howard Dean ran for president, Phish broke up and reunited, and someone from this state actually became a professional hockey player. There was somethin' about gay people, too. Oh, well. It'll come back to me. Always does, after I have a cup of coffee and stick my head in the freezer for fifteen minutes. Hang on . . .

For the record

Here is a list of Vermont's famous symbols and other fascinating facts:

Origin of name: *Vermont*, from the French vert mont, meaning "green mountain with a cell tower on top."

Official language: Glottal stop.

Demonym: Vermonner (and don't you forget it)

State song: "These Green Mountains," by Diane Martin and Rita Buglass Gluck. (It was "Hail, Vermont" by Josephine Hovey Perry of Barre, until May 22, 2000. My vote went to "Copacabana," but what do I know?)

Unofficial favorite state song: "Moonlight in Vermont" (Which I actually saw Willie Nelson perform live in Shelburne on a hot, summer night in . . . in . . . well, it was after 2000. Frickin' Grateful Dead!)

State beverage: milk (you were expecting Tang, maybe?)

State pie: apple (hot, with ice cream and Cabot cheese)

State mammal: Vermont redneck

State fish: the governor

State rock: the one where I smoked cigars on Lake Willoughby when I was in college

State tree: Aunt Jemima

State motto: Freedom and unity and Ben & Jerry's.

State bird: Hermit thrush (a close relation to the Maine state bird, Stephen King)

Major industries: farming, manufacturing, tourism, and teasing tourists

Bordering states: New York, New Hampshire, Massachusetts, and insanity

Some other big doin's that changed vermont

1. Construction of Interstate 89.
2. Native Vermonters realize the interstate leads to lots of upstreets.
3. 1927 flood.
4. 1927 is a banner year for Vermont mop salesmen.
5. In 1962, the state elects its first Democratic governor in 110 years, Phil Hoff. The GOP naps until 1969.
6. State legislators pass the Land Use and Development Act—commonly known as Act 250—in 1970. The law is designed to control development and preserve Vermont's green aesthetics. Ironically, it helps build an unwieldy sprawl of state bureaucracy chock-full of environmental agencies and non-profits, which are led primarily by—you guessed it—transplants.
7. The rise of the ski areas in 1934.
8. The fall of the family farm.
9. Madeleine Kunin is elected Vermont's first female governor in 1984. The historic "Estrogen Room" opens at the Vermont Statehouse. Kunin goes on to be President Clinton's deputy education secretary and U.S. ambassador to Switzerland.
10. Chittenden County booms. Everyone hears it.

Vermont firsts

For such a tiny state, Vermont often stands out on the national map. Besides being the first state to outlaw slavery, give a college degree to an African American (Alexander Twilight, Middlebury College, 1823), and join the Union after the original thirteen colonial states, Vermont boasts these other famous firsts:

- Woodstock introduced the nation to its first ski tow.
- The nation's first canal was built in Bellows Falls, 1802.
- Norwich University, the nation's first private military school, was established in Vermont and offered the country's first civil engineering course. Norwich also offered the first air traffic regulation course, in 1934.
- The nation's first normal school was founded in Concord in 1823. Every other school established in Vermont after that was considered abnormal.
- The American flag, featuring the stars and stripes, was first used in battle in Vermont.
- The first and longest alpine slide in North America is at Bromley ski area, in Peru. As in, Peru, Vermont, not the Peru that rests between Ecuador and Colombia. Cuz that's in South America now, ain't it, geography buffs?
- Wilson "Snowflake" Bentley, of Jericho, was the first person to photograph snowflakes.
- The nation's first chairlift was used in 1940, on Mount Mansfield. Not coincidentally, this was also the year that the first Vermont skier took a face plant while coming off a chairlift.
- Burlington physician H. Nelson Jackson was the first person to travel cross-country in a car. He started from San Francisco in 1903 and took lots and lots of Dramamine along the way.
- Isaac Underhill started the nation's first marble quarry in East Dorset, 1785.
- Scottish immigrant William F. Milne created the first Boy Scout troop while living in Barre, in 1909.
- Senator Warren Austin, of Burlington, was America's first ambassador to the United Nations.
- Ida M. Fuller, of Ludlow, was the first American to receive

Social Security benefits—$22.54 on January 31, 1940. (She easily remembered her Social Security number: 00-000-001.)

- The first postage stamp used in the U.S. was made in Brattleboro, 1846.
- Vermont was the first state to pass an absentee voting law, in 1896.
- Vermont had the first French-Catholic parish in America.
- Landmark College, in Putney, opened in 1985 as the country's first college specifically designed for dyslexics. The banner at the grand opening read WELCOME LANDMARK TO.
- Vermont was first with a state symphony orchestra.

And now I'll get all H. G. Wells on you and travel back to April 2009. While Vermont's Republican lawmakers worked diligently to convince their constituents that they could somehow flip the lagging economy, Democrats spent much of that session crafting a bill that would make Vermont the first state in the nation to legalize same-sex marriage through legislative action.

And it happened.

First, the Vermont Senate approved it. Then the Vermont House approved it under the shadow that GOP governor Jim Douglas would veto it. Upon passage, the House did not have the votes to override Douglas's veto.

But it did—by one vote.

A few other footnotes in Vermont history

Before we return to some stories—Yessssss!—here are a few other footnotes in Vermont history:

a. Vermont was the original home of the fictional villain Simon Legree in the novel *Uncle Tom's Cabin*.

b. Vermont was also the home of Dick Loudon, Bob Newhart's character on the 1980s sitcom, *Newhart*. All action supposedly took place in Vermont and featured three Vermont rednecks: Larry, Darryl, and Darryl. (Hi, I'm Larry. This is my brother, Darryl. And this is my other brother, Darryl. Classic.)

c. Vermont was the home of Pollyanna and her Aunt Polly in the novel *Pollyanna*.

d. In the first seasons of *M*A*S*H**, Alan Alda's character, Hawkeye Pierce, was from Vermont, though in later seasons he called Crabapple Cove, Maine, his home.

e. In the Marvel Comics shared universe, Vermont is home of the superhero team The Garrison.

f. Famous French explorer Jacques Cousteau learned to dive when he was ten while attending a summer school at Harvey's Lake in West Barnet.

g. David Dellinger, one of the Chicago Seven, lived in Peacham, for many years.

h. The films *Funny Farm* (Chevy Chase); *Baby Boom* (Diane Keaton); *The Cider House Rules* (Michael Caine); *The Spitfire Grill* (Ellen Burstyn); *What Lies Beneath* (Harrison Ford, Michelle Pfeiffer); *Me, Myself & Irene* (Jim Carrey, Renee Zellwegger), and *A Stranger in the Kingdom* (Martin Sheen) were all filmed in Vermont. And who could forget Vermont's famous connection to the Bing Crosby/Danny Kaye vehicle, *White Christmas*?

i. There is no "I." Just move on.

3

Modern-Day Politics and Government

No matter where you live—Alaska, Alabama, New York, North Dakota—you've inevitably heard the terms used to refer to Vermont folks.

"Crunchy granola eaters."

"Tree huggers."

"Liberals."

We have a strange and unique mix of conservatives and liberals here. We were a Red State. Now, we're Blue. Me? I'm color-blind. (That means I'm Independent, a color-blind voter.)

Why, though, does the rest of the country think we're a bunch of wacky, pot-smoking commies? Just because we have the nation's only Independent congressman? And because he doesn't comb his hair? Is it because our nation's last Republican president wouldn't even visit us during his eight years in office, even though he visited every other state in the Union? Is it because there was a small movement afoot in 2007 that called for Vermont to secede from the union?

Is it because we let gays tie the knot? Is it because students still demonstrate outside the president's office at the state's largest university? Is it because our state legislature—150 in the House, 30 in the Senate—is directed primarily by transplants and retirees who moved here to help the poor lil' rednecks run their state?

I'm not sure. All I know is right now I really have to go find my bong.

Local control

No, it's not the name of a struggling punk band that plays at Higher Ground in South Burlington, one of the state's best music venues. "Local control" is what Vermonters pride themselves on, in terms of governance. Vermonters don't take too kindly to state or federal mandates, especially when those mandates don't come with any money attached.

Vermont has two senators and one representative in the U.S. Congress. We have a General Assembly, a governor, a Supreme Court, and a small state capital (the only one in America sans a McDonald's, mind you).

However, the real strength in Vermont government lies in its three types of incorporated municipalities: towns, cities, and villages. Selectmen run towns. Aldermen run cities. Trustees run villages. And taxpayers run from all three. Taxpayers do, however, have a big say in town policy and spending: Their voice is called "Town Meeting," and not the kind of meeting where John McCain takes off his expensive suit coat, rolls up his sleeves, and calls us all his "friends," even though he's never bought us lunch. Or a beer.

Vermont's Town Meeting Day is held on the first Tuesday of each March and is declared a state holiday. At Town Meeting, residents conduct important business, such as potluck dinners,

raffles, and bake sales. Oh, yeah, they also elect municipal offi-
cers and adopt municipal and school budgets.

One-term "moderators" conduct the Town Meeting,
although this position has become less prominent with the
recent trend in towns moving to Australian ballot, which means
everyone votes from atop a kangaroo. Primarily, the moderator
keeps the meeting smooth, ensures civil civic debate, and
reviews the "warning"—the Town Meeting to-do list. Many
towns mail their warning to each resident as part of the annual
report, but you only get one warning, and if you lose it, the
town puts you in time-out.

Like Champ, skiing, and maple syrup, Town Meeting is a staple of Vermont. Once asked to name his favorite place in
America, the late Charles Kuralt, host of CBS's *On the Road*,
said it would be Strafford, Vermont, on Town Meeting Day.
Thomas Jefferson once called Town Meeting "the wisest inven-
tion ever devised by the wit of man for the perfect exercise of
self-government." Well put, for a straight man in a powdered
wig.

How powerful is Town Meeting? Picture Governor Madeline
Kunin standing outside Duxbury Town Hall in the late 1980s,
with light snow falling in the parking lot. Why would Vermont's
governor stand outside in the snow, alone, on the first Tuesday
in March?

She was waiting for the residents to finish voting on whether
she should be allowed to speak. Even the president of the
United States, should he or she deign to come here, needs
town permission to speak at Town Meeting. Now that's local
control.

Some other fun facts about Town Meeting:

- In the early 1980s, Vermont was in the national and international spotlight for its Town Meeting votes that requested a nuclear weapons test ban treaty.
- On average, towns that have a population of 2,500 or less see 20 percent of their registered voters at Town Meeting. In those same towns, about 40 percent of those in attendance will participate verbally in the meeting. On the other hand, towns with 2,500 people or less will often get 85 percent attendance at a rally to save the whales, when Vermont isn't even near the ocean.
- If you want an item placed on the Town Meeting warning, you only need to submit a petition that has support from 5 percent of registered voters. For example, if 5 percent of registered voters want fairies to sprinkle magic dust on icy, wintry roads in order to cut costs on road salt, they need only petition for that item to go on the Town Meeting ballot. And then run from the men in straitjackets.
- In 1936, on Town Meeting Day, Vermonters said "no"— 42,873 to 30,795—to building The Green Mountain Parkway, a highway that would have run alongside the Green Mountains.
- There is no specified percentage of voters necessary to constitute a quorum at Town Meeting. "But," a buddy once asked me, "what happens if you only get two participants and they are on opposite sides?"
  I sicced Champ on him.
  I have other buddies.
- It takes two-thirds of voters present to suspend the rules at Town Meeting. Rules could be suspended for a variety of reasons, such as a need to rearrange the articles on the

town warning. When the rules are acting out in class, they aren't suspended; instead, they earn detention with Molly Ringwald, Judd Nelson, and Emilio Estevez. Not so bad.

- In 1974, Thetford made national news by becoming the first town in America to request Richard Nixon's impeachment, on Town Meeting Day.
- Town Meeting attendance is generally lower when the sessions are held at night.
- My favorite Town Meeting dish ever was this meat pie I ate during a Bakersfield meeting in the late 1990s. I'll never frickin' forget it. Wish I remembered who made it. I sure could use some right about now.

4

Vocabulary

The way we talk is frickin' important. Language is the road map of culture. At least that's what I learned from Google just now.

If that adage is true—and since it came off the Internet, it must be—there are several coffee stains on Vermont's linguistic road map that you should know about before we proceed. Learn them. We native Vermonters always know when visitors don't, and then we are less welcoming. If we have to look at your white license plates, you have to learn how we talk. This is what we call "fair." Moreover, you won't get the most out of your visit to our state if you can't tell what the heck we're saying.

Study the following before you come:

Mysteriously, Vermonters think the letter "T" went the way of the dinosaur (except for Champ), especially when partnered with the letter "N." We swallow our T's, a speech pattern known as the glottal stop. My hometown is prounounced "Swah'in," not "Swanton," and my birthplace is "Snobbins," not "St. Albans." Instead of saying "kitten," we say "kih'en."

Ironically, we don't say "gloh'al stop."

Also note that it's pronounced "Innernet," not "Internet." This is because native Vermonters don't "inter" anything. We always "inner" whatever we think needs inner-ing.

We don't like taking the innerstate, but we do.

We inneract with our neighbors from our porches.

The opposing team innercepts the puck. Dammit!

When we sneeze in church, we're innerrupting.

People with white license plates are innerfering.

And no matter how many cutesy, folksy times you've heard it said or seen it written—all phonetically accurate and what-not—we are not, never have been, and never will be "Vermontahs."

We're Vermonners.

Which leads me to our next verbal language rule: Droppin' the "g" from "ing," a staple of New England vernacular, not just Vermont. In many cases, however, Vermonters combine the g-drop and glottal stop.

"Hey, Travis, you wanna goda the truck pull and see if Jim's there?"

"Nah. I sure as hell ain' innerested in seein' him. I'm gonna wanna stay here and git on the Innernet. You goin'?"

"Yup. Maybe I'll go lookin' fer Jim."

"Oh, that's real frickin' nice, Randy! After what he said to me last weekend at the bar? What's ailin' you?"

"Hey, I ain't gonna do nothin' but talk to 'im."

"You sure?"

"Sure."

"Alright, then. Love ya."

"Yeah. You, too. Fricker."

(You smarter types will notice I just foreshadowed gay marriage.)

Though not relegated to Vermont—or even invented here, though we like to think so—"frickin" and "fricker" are common Vermont euphemisms for curse words. "Frickin'" is derived from its more commonly known root, "friggin'," but I could also be making that up.

Sometimes, an "A" is added for emphasis.

"Frickin' A, Bill, why ain'choo snowblowin' 'at driveway yet?"

Someone told me they once saw a T-shirt that had Jesus on the front, sitting at his carpenter's bench and screaming "Elvis H. Presley!" because he smacked his thumb with a hammer.

I want that shirt. In black. A medium. (Hint, hint . . .)

Instead of using the Lord's name in vain—though it does happen, especially when the sugaring isn't too good—Vermonters often activate one of three phrases they view as acceptable substitutes.

"Keeey-RIST!"

"Ah, fer cripes' sakes."

And the most popular: "Jeezum Crow!"

OK. Go ahead. Get it out of your system. "The Jeezum Crow is the Vermont state bird!" Ha. Ha. Ha. Yeah, none of us have heard THAT before.

Frickers.

Here are some other highlights of our vernacular, in no particular order:

Pronouncing the hard "i" as "oy": "Driver" becomes "droyver." You don't "ride" your snowmobile, you "royd" it. And the town adjacent to Swanton? It's not "Highgate." It's "Oygate."

Putting an object pronoun at the end of a sentence or question, when speaking in third person:

"What's he doin' there, him?"

"Did you put that there, you?"

"I can't do a damn thing right, me."

(MeMe Laroche, my maternal grandmother, was good at this. If she couldn't answer a question, she'd say, "I dunno, me.")

Overuse of "says" in storytelling: "So I says to him, I says, 'Hey, if you think yer gettin' some o' this, yer gonna have to do a lot more 'n buy me a few Buds.' And he says to me, he says, 'Fine. Where's the frickin' tequila?' And I says, 'Now yer talkin'.' "

Surprisingly effective use of double negatives:

"I like the color blue."

"Yeah. So don't I."

"This car is red."

"So isn't this one."

"This meat is froze."

"Well, then, stick it in the microwave and unthaw it."

(I'm unsure if "unthaw" fits in this category, but Mom says it all the time. And I always says to her, I says, "That ain't how you say that." And she says to me, she says, "Stop correctin' me." Then it gets ugly.)

all set: has various uses, but, generally speaking, means, "Are you ready?" (the interrogative form) or, "I have everything I need" (the declarative form).

"You need any more coffee, Bruce, or are you all set?"

"Nope, nope, nope. I'm all set."

doin's: events that are taking place in the community, with your family, or otherwise in your social life. Grandma Thompson is particularly adept with the use of the word "doin's."

"Hey, Le-in, what were the doin's today in the high school parking lot? It was all over the scanner."

(Note: Vermonters, particularly senior citizens, keep radio frequency scanners in their homes to follow the action of their local police, fire, and rescue squads. Don't ask why. Just accept it, and move on.)

not too awful bad: A Vermonter's way of tellin' you he's happy, that life is good.

"How's it goin', Harold?"

"Oh, not too awful bad. Nooot tooo baaad."

(A prolonged pronunciation in a repetition of the "not too awful bad," as seen above, often sparks welcome follow-up questions about your life. In other words: It's a good way to get people innerested in your doin's.)

air: common substitute for the word "there," especially among hunters, fishermen, and other outdoorsmen.

"So, uh, yesterday, air, I was out inna woods, air. And I saw two frickin' bucks, air, just starin' right at me, air."

"No frickin' way! Joo git a shot off, air?"

"Nope. Snowfleas got in my eyes, air."

Note: "Air" is also used to substitute "care" in the phrase "take care." When Vermonters wish others well, they say, "Take air."

Green Mountain Hannaford's Syndrome: The practice of adding an apostrophe "s" to singular commercial establishments, thus making them possessive.

Hannaford = "Hannaford's"

KMart = "KMart's"

Costco = "Costco's."

"Hey, Suzy, you wanna go to Costco's with the kids tomorrow? I wanna get some of them big muffins."

Along these same lines, everyone in Vermont who wears a uniform for a sheriff's department is a "sheriff." Deputies do not exist among native Vermonters.

"Oh, yeah! Keep it up, an' I'm callin' the sheriffs!"

downstreet: used when going to town, or a city

"Welp, I'm outta orange juice. Gotta go downstreet."

"Upstreet" is also acceptable.

down cellar: the basement of a house

"Have you seen my shit kickers?"

"They were down cellar, last I knew."

Curiously, there is no "up attic."

yee-ellow: how a Vermonter answers the phone. (We've gone over this already. You paying attention?)

yut: affirmative, as in "yes"

upta: up to

"Hey, Fred. Watchya upta?"

tryta: try to

"I'd like to go, but I'm not sure I can. I'll sure tryta."

flatlander: generic term for non-native Vermonter, but we'll get more into this later. Or at least tryta.

suttin: something

"I dunno 'bout you, Bill, but I think that new waitress at Jana's Cupboard is suttin'."

"Yut, yut. She is."

fer once and for all: the end of it

"You git my little girl knocked up, and yer marryin' her, fer once and for all."

frun: from

"If you ain't gittin' none frun him, you sure as hell ain't gettin' none frun me."

on accident: accidentally

"Dad? I just ran over the dog with the four-wheeler. He's alive, but it don't look too good. I promise it was on accident!"

nuther: another

"Yeah, I'm prob'ly gonna leave after two-nuther beers and three-nuther cigarettes."

you'll have that: a Vermonter's version of "shit happens"

I'll let you go: Strangely, this is how a Vermonter lets the person on the other end of the phone know he's had enough of the conversation, or that his popcorn is burning in the microwave.

"Welp, I'll let you go."

"It makes no sense," a friend in South Carolina once pointed out to me. "By saying, 'I'll let you go,' you're telling the person on the other end of the line that you need to go. Shouldn't you say, 'Can you let me go?' instead?"

Right then, I hung up on her.

gararge: Where you store your car, your snowmobile, or where you sneak cigarettes when your wife ain't looking.

go it: A Vermonter's passive-aggressive way of telling someone he really doesn't want someone else to do something risky or dangerous. Parents often use "go it" on their teenagers.

"Fine. You wanna jump off John's Bridge with all your friends? Go it, ya damn fool."

that'll learn ya: "I hope you learned a lesson." Primarily used in subsequence to "go it."

"So ya went and broke your arm while jumpin' off John's Bridge, eh? That'll learn ya."

I set right there and waited: used to express patience.

"So, after the snowfleas got in yer eyes, air, what happened?"

"Frickin' deer left."

"Crap. You leave, too?"

"Nope. I set right there and waited."

jeet yet?: Are you hungry?

Typically used when a friend, relative, or neighbor inevitably arrives at your doorstep during a meal, whether it's breakfast, dinner, or supper. (Vermonters don't eat "breakfast, lunch, and dinner." We have "breakfast, dinner, and supper." Sometimes all at once.)

ja-gitit: Did you get it?"

a real turd floater: a heavy rainstorm

crick: a "brook" or "creek"

Riiiing! Riiing!

"Yee-ellow!"

"Hey, it's Brian, from upstreet. Skatin's good on the crick. I was thinkin' about takin' the boys. You an' Zach wanna come?"

i-deer: idea

"You know what, Brian? That ain' a bad i-deer."

"Yut! I know it!"

I know it: see "i-deer"

Why yass!: of course

"You think that i-deer's gonna work?"

"Why yass!"

fusstrated: frustrated

Magnabucks: A biweekly lottery game played in Maine, New Hampshire, and Vermont, where players pick six numbers from a field of forty-two and take chances at winning various prizes, based on how many of their numbers match the winning six.

"Hey, Jean, you bought your Magnabucks ticket yet this week? Frickin' jackpot's HUGE!"

"Why yass! You kiddin'? I'm winnin' that sucker, fer cripes' sake!"

(Also known as "Tri-State Megabucks.")

creamies or creemees: soft-serve ice cream, often used as a summertime bribery tool for parents with naughty children

"That's it, Henry! We ain't gittin' no cree-mee! Not the way yer actin'!"

fudgicle: a frozen, chocolate confection on a stick, known everywhere else as a "Fudgesicle"

"No, Henry, you ain't havin' no fudgicle, either!"

sucker: lollipop

"Henry! HENRY! Stop runnin' around with that sucker, 'fore you choke on it!"

usetuvit: used to it

"Well, guess what, Mikey! Ma says you ain't allowed in my room, so you better git usetuvit!"

coontuv, shoontuv, woontuv: could not have, should not have and would not have

"He coontuv gone over there, not drunk like that."

"Well, he did. And he shoontuv."

"I know I woontuv."

Similarly, cootuv, shootuv, and wootuv.

wount up: Excited, as in wound up

"Fer cripes' sake, Harold, don't go danglin' yer raw venison liver in fron' o' the dog like 'at. Yer gonna git 'im all wount up."

member: remember, recall.

"Hey, Larry, you member years ago, when we belonged to the Elks, we had that member who got his member caught in the vendin' machine when he was tryin' to git some M&Ms? You member that member?"

"Why yass! Gilbert Gilmond! I member him!"

"Yup! Gilbert Gilmond! Keey-rist, how'd you member that member?"

"I dunno, me."

minds me: reminds me (a close relative of "member")

"Yeah, I know, I seen 'im with her yesterday. Hey, that 'minds me, do you think your brother would go out with me? I don't care if he's fifteen. It's legal."

them ones: those

"Hey, gimme some o' them ones, wouldja?"

your guyses: yours

"I ain't too sure I got enough night crawlers or beer to last me the whole day. If I don't, can I have some of your guyses?"

cuzzint: any one of your parents' siblings' children.

You can talk to your cuzzint. You can play Monopoly with your cuzzint. You can take your cuzzint to your senior prom, if you want. But you shouldn't ever have sex with your cuzzint, or marry her.

But you know what?

You'll have that.

acouple-three: two or three

pret-near: almost

I'm right out straight: I'm busy.

so don't I: I do, too.

"I got me some o' them ones."

"So don't I."

hard tellin', not knowin': We'll have to wait and see."

"I think it's gonna rain today, Warren. Check out those clouds."

"Could be, Sandy. Hard tellin', not knowin'."

susty: the art of being pretentiously sustainable, usually applied to college students who come from Massachusetts to Vermont and believe that this somehow makes them an environmental god or goddess because they can buy farm-fresh, local, organic, sustainably grown, grass-fed, free-range produce with their daddy's big corporation money.

wassadallabout: "What's the meaning behind that?" or "Why is that happening?"

"I pret-near won the Magnabucks last week! Every number I had was two off from each o' the six winnin' numbers. Wassadallabout?"

Okay, that should do. Remember, study the above before you head our way, so you'll be all set when you arrive.

5

Vermonters Declassified

Vermont basically has two types of people: natives and those from away. Within those two categories, though, there are subsets. First, a look at the natives.

Natives

Rednecks

Vermont rednecks are natives born and raised. My dear friend and native Vermonter Suzy says, "Vermont rednecks learned 'redneck' from their ancestors. Then they adapted their ingrained redneck patterns and nuances to fit the times. Somewhat. Because Vermont rednecks are old-fashioned. Vermont rednecks don't drive fancy, foreign cars. Vermont red-necks do not surf the Internet, shop in Burlington, drink tea if it's not iced, listen to hip hop or jazz or classical music, or fly." (At least on an airplane. But landing gear on a snowmobile is essential in Vermont.)

"The Vermont redneck is a carefully crafted entity," Suzy adds. "And—probably most important—their four-wheelers are loud. Key. Very key."

During Suzy's adolescence in St. Albans—where, if you were sans a vehicle, you were ska-rood—a Friday or Saturday night might entail a bottle of Boone's Farm and cow tipping, which Suzy has witnessed but never done.

That's Vermont redneck.

As a young adult, when Suzy had an apartment in Highgate, she and some friends caught a small bass and gave it a ten-gallon home in her living room. On summer nights, Suzy and pals swarmed her porch for moths, June bugs and other winged ugliness that surrounded the porchlight. Then, they took turns feeding the bugs to the bass and cheered when he surfaced to nab his prey. His name was Buster—Buster Bass.

That's also Vermont redneck.

Suzy says the most Vermont redneck behavior she's ever seen—and that says a lot, coming from a native—also occurred while she was in high school. Suzy befriended the Clark brothers. Farmers. Trustworthy guys. And fun—"So much redneck fun," Suzy says. (Most rednecks are fun.) Often, she and the Clark brothers piled into the Clarkmobile, drove forever, and turned left when there was no other choice. The Clarkmobile had mechanical issues and no brakes, but it did have a license plate that said BADENUFF.

That, too, is Vermont redneck.

One year the Clarks fell on hard times, according to Suzy, and their house went under auction—not because the Clarks are lazy or irresponsible people, but because, well, you'll have that.

On the last day the Clarks were in their home, one of the brothers decided he'd leave the new owners a generous housewarming gift. He opened a heating grate in the floor and hid a dead fish underneath it, and then optimistically looked at the next steps in his struggling family's life.

How to tell if someone's a redneck Vermonter

- Their idea of a traffic jam is ten cars stuck behind a slow shit-spreader.
- Their idea of "vacation" means going to Burlington.
- They measure distance in hours.
- They know several people who have struck a moose with a car—more than once.
- They use a down comforter in July.
- They wear hunter-orange at social events.
- They install security lights on their house and garage and leave both unlocked at bedtime.
- Their major food groups are: beer, venison, beer, fish, and Chinese food. With beer.
- They carry jumper cables in their cars, and their girlfriends use them.
- They think sexy lingerie is tube socks and flannel PJs.
- It takes them three hours to go to the store for one item, because they see at least three people they know—one conversation per hour.
- They call it "Valentime's Day."

That, amigos, is very, very Vermont redneck. Still, it's not as Vermont redneck as Vermont redneck gets.

In September 2008, Trevor and Crystal Gingras threw a highly publicized Vermont-redneck wedding in Sheldon, a tight-knit, Franklin County farming community with a nudists' campground (more on that later, as promised).

At the wedding, which a local TV station featured on its nightly newscast, the newlyweds (who—surprise, surprise— fell in love at a stock-car race track) decorated the reception hall with mounted deer heads and vases made from antlers. The bridesmaids wore camouflage. The groomsmen chewed and spit tobacco. The ring was made of candy.

"Everything I own is made of camouflage," Trevor Gingras told a TV reporter, "so I went with it."

That's pretty frickin' Vermont redneck right there.

But it's still not as Vermont redneck as Vermont redneck can get.

That would be lawn sale-ing.

Lawn sale-ing is the act of hitting many lawn sales in one day, thanks to classifieds listings in the local newspaper. Lawn sale-ing is a sport—a true, Vermont redneck event.

There are actually three varieties of sale-ing in Vermont: lawn, porch, and garage. (Vermont rednecks never say "tag sale," by the way.)

Suzy (Buster Bass's owner) and her sister Marcie went lawn sale-ing one afternoon and found the Holy Grail of lawn sale items—a blue glass cologne bottle shaped like a gun. This one had a holster. Bonus. Marcie picked it up. Immediately, the woman selling her used wares sprang from her webbed lawn chair (the boilerplate throne for every lawn, porch, or garage sale merchant).

"Ohhhh, yaaayyyy!" the woman screamed. "I've been waiting for someone to pick that up all day!"

Vermont rednecks take sale-ing seriously. So much so, that St. Albans City adopted a sale-ing ordinance: "No person shall operate or maintain a lawn/porch/garage sale or any combination thereof within the city limits without first obtaining a license from the city clerk."

Otherwise, "people would sell stuff out on their lawns all summer," says Dianna Baraby, who was St. Albans city clerk when aldermen adopted the ordinance.

The permit comes with several conditions: The license is valid for ten days; no one can obtain more than four licenses per calendar year, and sale-ors must shut down their sales for seven days before they can acquire a new license. First and second licenses are free. The third license is ten dollars; the fourth is fifteen dollars. And, yes, there are penalties: "Any person who shall violate any of the provisions of this subsection relating to the operation of a lawn/porch/garage sale shall be subject to a fine not exceeding fifteen dollars and each day's violation shall be deemed a separate offense."

 There is only one machine, master, and mentor—the M-cubed of garage sale-ing, as I mentioned earlier: Grandpa Thompson. At a young age, he turned buying and reselling into a science and art. Never go to a garage, yard, or porch sale and purchase anything you think you need, or that might look good on your coffee table, he advises. He rarely keeps what he buys. Instead, he meticulously scours other garage, porch, and yard sales for items he knows—he somehow KNOWS—he can turn around and sell for profit.

His forte? Lamps. When he makes money on a garage sale lamp, he acts like he just sold a bridge. Cheap.

"You know how much I paid for this one, Le-urn?" he whispers covertly, with a Sicilian hit man's glint in his eye.

"How much?"

"Two dollars. Know how much I sold it for?"

I shake my head.

"Three." (My other French-Canadian grandpa would have said "tree.")

Grandpa Thompson—consummate garage sale-or.

Yes—fifteen bucks. That's a whole lot of gun-shaped cologne bottles.

Hipbillies

I'm at On the Run, a quick stop/gas station/free Wi-Fi workplace near the intersection of Route 104 and the Interstate 89 access road in St. Albans Town. A rabbi sits in front of me, devouring a slice of cheese pizza. Two U.S. Border Patrol agents sit behind me, dressed in their government-issued dark blues and talking shop. Outside, motorists fill their cars, which have license plates of all colors. Green. White. I even see a Rhode Island. Rare around here.

Here, at On the Run, it's hard to tell who's a native and who's not—unless you know someone. Then it's easy. Otherwise, it's all guessing, all the time. I do some of my writing here because I love to watch people. On the Run is a people-watcher's winning Magnabucks ticket.

We've already covered the first type of native—the redneck. The second is the hipbilly.

Vermont's hipbillies used to be hardest for me to define, until I met my hipbilly friend Becky, a Montgomery-born waitress at (warning: shameless plug) Mimmo's Restaurant in St. Albans. When I met Becky, she was earning her math degree at Johnson State College. (You can do a lot with a math degree in this country. English degrees land you in the middle of a sentence like this one.)

"There are Vermonters who have some hippie and some hillbilly in them," Becky once told me. "They can be redneck. And they can be hip."

"They're 'hipbillies,' " I said. Becky high-fived me. Twice. Which I guess made it a high-ten.

With her math-oriented mind, Becky quickly rattled off the complex set of constants, variables, and equations that eventually led us to this result—the hipbilly.

Hippies + Hillbillies = Hipbillies

A hipbilly must—must—be native, with the required threshold of generational dirt naps within state boundaries. They have Vermont redneck in their blood and unabashedly display it at family pig roasts—where they actually eat pig—but then conceal it at places where rednecks wouldn't be caught dead, such as Barnes & Noble or a pricey Burlington bistro. Hipbillies step outside country music. They watch indie films. They know what's happening in India. They aren't afraid to drink cheap beer in an ice-fishing shanty on a warm January afternoon, or ride a four-wheeler down a dirt road in Bakersfield. Without a helmet. Hipbillies are chameleons.

Typically, Vermont rednecks like the Red Sox and hipbillies dig the Cubs. Or the Dodgers. And Miles Davis. They mix, mingle, and make friends with all kinds of Vermonters, even non-natives!

Transplants

If natives make up the first major classification of Vermonters, the second classification is made up of, you guessed it, non-natives. Many Vermonters, but not me, toss around the term "flatlander" quite a bit when talking about those from out of state. According to www.vermonter.com, the term describes "a person who visits the state or lives here that brings negative qualities from their home to our state. It is a person who is unfamiliar with traditional Vermont ways."

Native Vermonter Nathan Mansfield famously described flatlanders as "thinking they can meld their beliefs of what Vermont is into our reality." Hal Goldman, a Vermont attorney, once blamed the state's problems on flatlanders. "Hundreds of

A Vermont farmer in Addison County was overseeing his herd in a remote pasture, when a brand-new, tomato-hued BMW shot from a dust cloud and straight toward him.

The driver was a young man, probably in his late forties—young to the farmer. He wore a Brioni suit, Gucci shoes, Ray-Ban sunglasses, and a YSL tie. (That's "Yves Saint Laurent," for those of you who liken Carhartt to Versace.)

The hotshot stopped, leaned out his window, and asked the farmer, "If I tell you how many cows and calves you have in your herd, will you give me a calf?"

The farmer looked at the hotshot. Then at his herd. Then at the tomato-red BMW. Then back at his herd. Then at the hotshot.

"Sure," he said. "Why not?"

The hotshot parked his car, whipped out his Dell notebook computer, connected it to his Cingular RAZR V3 cell phone, and surfed to a NASA page on the Internet, where he called up a GPS satellite to get an exact fix on his location, which he then fed to another NASA satellite that scanned the area in an ultra-high-resolution photo.

The farmer watched.

The hotshot then opened the picture in Adobe Photoshop and exported it to an image-processing facility in Hamburg, Germany. Within seconds, he received e-mail on his Palm Pilot that said the image was processed, and the data stored. He then accessed an MS SQL Server database through an ODBC-connected Excel spreadsheet with e-mail on his Blackberry, and, after a few minutes, received a response.

The farmer kept watching.

Finally, the hotshot printed a full-color, 150-page report on his high-tech, miniaturized HP Laser Jet printer. He then turned to the farmer, smirked, and said, "You have exactly one thousand five hundred and eighty-six cows and calves."

"That's right!" the farmer exclaimed, slightly impressed. "Welp, I guess you git one o' my calves."

> The farmer smacked his forehead as he watched the hotshot lift one of the animals and stuff it into his trunk.
> "Hey," the farmer said. "If I can tell you exactly what your business is, will you give that animal back?"
> The hotshot thought for a moment. "Alright. Deal."
> "You're a U.S. congressman," the farmer declared.
> "Wow! That's right! But . . . how did you guess?"
> "No guessin' required," the farmer said. "You showed up here, even though nobody called you. You want to get paid for an answer I already knew, for a question I didn't even ask. You tried to show me how much smarter than me you are, and you don't know a thing about cows. Now . . .
> " . . . gimme back my dog."

thousands of highly educated, well-off people invaded a state with a unique culture and history," he told Vermonter.com. "They seized control of its resources and institutions, demeaned the landscape, and drove many of the natives from their homes as a result of their activities.

"If this happened in Africa, the same people would call it colonialism. In Vermont, it's called liberal chic."

Not every out-of-stater who sets foot in Vermont is from a "flat land." Some are from mountainous areas outside Vermont; more are from cities. So, to me, the term "flatlander"— although not entirely out of line, by any means—is misleading in certain situations.

For our purposes, I have a different definition of a "flat-lander." Flatlanders pass through. Transplants stay.

Transplants are commonly seen as deep-pocketed, well-educated (just ask them) creatures from urban or suburban U.S.A. who seek quieter lives in great, green, rural Vermont.

Many transplants settled in Vermont during the North American "back-to-the-land movement" of the 1960s and 1970s, when young people migrated from cities to rural areas. (Rumor has it James Taylor—yes, "Sweet Baby James" Taylor— lived in Fairfield during this period.)

Upon arrival, these young transplants wielded self-suffi- ciency to build their own homes—or, as was often the case, to form communes—produce their own food, and collect modest income in the cottage industries. Over time, these same trans- plants inherited affluence and raised trust-fund babies in six- figure homes they built on the same tract of land they tried to preserve when their names were "Moon Mother" and "Grass Whisperer."

We still have hippies here. Just look for the people that look like Willie Nelson and poke them. If they hug you, you've found a hippie. If something else happens, you've accidentally poked a redneck that looks like a hippie. Then, I suggest run- ning. Fast.

My friend Clarice, a transplant from Helena, Montana, says native Vermonters are generally xenophobes. (Doesn't it figure that someone from another state would move here and start tossing around words we can't spell, never mind pronounce? Whatever that word means, we ain't them.)

"People who've lived here all their lives seem to have a com- mon mistrust of flatlanders," Clarice says—wrongly, of course. To reiterate: We trust flatlanders, because they don't stick around, and we trust the money they drop in our state for cheese and Ben & Jerry's T-shirts. But the transplants? The transplants are the ones we watch at night. With binoculars.

"I think there are a lot of people, though, who come here from other states and want desperately to be considered

Vermonters," Clarice adds. "They work hard to shred the remnants of where they came from, and only begrudgingly admit where that was, if directly asked the question. They usually say apologetically, 'I came from wherever, but I've lived in Vermont for XX years.'

"The implication is that if they've been here long enough, they are real Vermonters. But the natives know that you must be several generations deep in order to be considered that."

If you were born outside Vermont, but live here, you'll never be a native, no matter how you assimilate yourself. True natives have at least ten generations under the ground. And counting.

Our first clue that you're a transplant? No glottal stop. So if you wanna fit in, you better get workin' on it.

Asked for her input on transplants for this book, my friend Wendy scratched her pretty noggin and said, "Transplant? I've lived here twenty years. I'm not a transplant."

"And where are you from?" I asked.

"Upstate New York."

Bzzz! Wrong answer. But thank you for playing.

So how does a transplant become a Vermonter?

Simple.

Legislative action.

Dr. William H. Bloom might be Vermont's most notable transplant. In January 2001, the Vermont General Assembly passed a resolution that named Dr. Bloom an honorary native Vermonter. It reads:

> Whereas, individuals who were born in the Green Mountain State are rightfully proud of their special status as native Vermonters, and

Transplants vs. Rednecks

- In the winter, transplants wear hand-woven toques, North Face jackets, and all-purpose boots that cost a monthly car payment for the average redneck.
  Rednecks wear flannel.
- Transplants like public entertainment—public radio, public television, and free waterfront concerts in Burlington during the summer.
  Rednecks dig a dirty demolition derby.
- Transplants ski.
  Rednecks snowmobile. (Yes, they made it a verb.)
- Transplant book collection: outdoor guides, historical and political biographies, and anything by Malcom Gladwell.
  Redneck book collection: Stephen King, John Grisham, and Michael Crichton. All in paperback. Because they make good beer coasters.
- Music at transplant wedding: live rockabilly.
  Music at redneck wedding: a sloshed DJ who routinely plays "Taking Care of Business," "Old Time Rock and Roll," and the Chicken Dance.
- Transplants fill their refrigerators and pantries with fresh goods from the nearby all-natural and organic market, where a box of rice costs twelve dollars and fifty cents.
  Rednecks skin squirrels.
- Transplants think they know how to save the land.
  Rednecks know the land. Personally.
- Transplants are lawyers.
  Rednecks are sheriffs.

Whereas, while a flatlander may reside in Vermont for nearly an entire lifetime, and make an indelible contribution to the quality of life in this state, a flatlander still has not earned the right to be called a native Vermonter, and

Whereas, although Dr. William Bloom did not actually enter this world within the geographic confines of Vermont, having been born at his parents' home in Granville, New York, he was, however, conceived in Poultney and, had it not been for a blizzard, would have been born at the Rutland Hospital, and . . .

. . . Whereas, Dr. Bloom renewed his ties to Vermont in October 2000 upon his appointment to the newly-formed Board of Visitors of Green Mountain College, and

Whereas, Dr. Bloom's lifelong love for Vermont, and the meteorological disturbance that prevented his birth in Rutland, as originally intended, are both persuasive reasons for awarding him status as an "honorary native Vermonter," now therefore be it RESOLVED BY THE SENATE AND HOUSE OF REPRESENTATIVES:

That the General Assembly extends the status of "honorary native Vermonter" to Dr. William H. Bloom.

See, Wendy? There's still hope—if you're cozy with any lawmakers. Otherwise, you're on your own.

Meanwhile, you can break transplants down into two types: those who assimilate to Vermont and accept it as it is (though it takes work), and those who come to escape city life but incessantly complain about the manure smell that emerges from the dairy farm adjacent to their new home, or about the poor cell phone coverage, or the lack of . . . well, you get it. And yet—they still stay. Why, we ask? Whyyyyyyyyy?

6

Famous Rednecks, Transplants, and Hipbillies

Vermont has its share of celebrities and ties to them, whether they are from here or just act like they are because Vermont is cool. These are the notables most associated with Vermont, starting with our heavy hitters.

Famous Vermonters

Ethan Allen

Born in Litchfield, Connecticut—NOT Vermont—in 1738, Allen moved to the territory that would become Vermont (in 1769) and organized the Green Mountain Boys, a volunteer militia. Allen was instrumental in the capture of Fort Ticonderoga from the British in May 1775. And he was probably drunk while he did it. He drank. A lot. (Ethan's younger brother, Ira, the Roger Clinton of his day, was also a Green Mountain Boy.)

The von Trapp Family

In 1938, Maria and Baron Georg von Trapp fled from Austria to Switzerland with their children and inspired the 1959 Broadway musical and 1965 film, *The Sound of Music*, starring Julie Andrews and Christopher Plummer. The family settled in

Supposedly, this is true: Samuel Clemens—writing as Mark Twain—made a decent living in his later years, touring the country and reading from his works to paying audiences. He elicited huge laughs with a fine-tuned delivery and built quite a successful venture. Passing through Vermont, he stopped to give a reading at a town hall. People filled the seats. Clemens stepped up to the lectern and began his program. Reaching the first line, which always drew a laugh, the audience instead greeted Clemens with silence. He stumbled but continued. At the next funny line? Silence. Again.

The pattern repeated through the lecture. By now, Clemens was sweating visibly and wondering what went wrong. At the end, he thanked the audience and received strong applause. He was perplexed.

As people filed out of the hall, Clemens slipped out the back door and hid in the shadows to overhear the comments of people leaving.

"So, what'd you think of him?" a woman asked her husband.

"That be the funniest man I ever heard," he said. "A couple times, sir, I almost laughed out loud."

Stowe and opened the landmark Trapp Family Lodge. Maria died in 1987, at age eighty-two. It was only after her death that the Vermont Fish and Wildlife Department would establish a permit-only system to shoot doe (a deer, a female deer).

Norman Rockwell

Sure, he was born in New York City; lots of famous people who live in Vermont are. Rockwell, however, is famous for his portraits of small-town New England life and lived in Arlington, from 1939 to 1953. Often, he used his Vermont neighbors as models.

Ben Cohen and Jerry Greenfield

The Ben and Jerry of Ben & Jerry's ice cream—the most famous Vermont product that doesn't drip from trees or teats.

Phish

The phamous, phour-man jam band phormed at the University oph Vermont in 1983 and perphormed phor more than twenty years, until they bid pharewell during a mud-covered two-day bash in Coventry. Phortunately phor phans, Phish reunited in 2009. Phish shows and snowphlakes have a common denominator: No two are alike.

Phred . . . I mean . . . Fred Tuttle

Fred lived a quiet life as a wise dairy farmer in Tunbridge until 1995, when filmmaker John O'Brien cast him as the lead in *Man with a Plan*, a mockumentary about a wise, salt-of-the-earth farmer who runs for Congress. Fred, who was nearly eighty during filming, became an unlikely celebrity, with appearances on *Late Night with Conan O'Brien* and articles in *The New York Times* and *The New Yorker*.

In 1998, Fred ran against multimillionaire Jack McMullen in the Republican U.S. Senate primary. During a televised debate, Fred peppered McMullen with humorous questions about Vermont facts.

"How many teats a Holstein got?" Fred asked.

"Six," McMullen said.

The correct answer: four.

Fred beat McMullen by ten percentage points and quickly endorsed Democratic incumbent Pat Leahy in the general election. Fred famously said he didn't want to win the race, because then he'd have to move to Washington, D.C. (Leahy, by this time, was 10,000 years old.)

Howard Dean

Arguably Vermont's most politically successful governor. Dr. Dean—he is a physician—served six two-year terms as governor, until he ran unsuccessfully for the 2004 Democratic presidential nomination.

Initially ranked eighth out of twelve Democratic contenders for the Oval Office, Dean's campaign gained steam. Al Gore endorsed him. So did Bill Bradley. And Paul Newman. And Robin Williams. Candidate Dean was on the cover of *The New Republic*, *Time*, and *Newsweek*.

And then it happened.

One can list all sorts of reasons for a failed presidential campaign, but many point to only one that ruined Dean. On January 19, 2004, Dean's campaign took a hit when he placed third behind John Kerry and John Edwards in the Iowa caucuses. At a subsequent rally, Dean was shouting over the cheers of his excited audience. Unfortunately for Dean, the crowd noise was filtered out for TV viewers, which left them hearing only one sound.

"YEAAAUUUGGGHHH!"

Dean found a new life as chairman of the Democratic National Party and employed the "50 State Strategy" during the 2008 election, aimed at making Democrats more competitive in traditionally conservative states. The result? Barack Obama became the nation's first black president. Democrats regained the White House.

And how did Obama repay Dean?

No cabinet post.

"YEAAAUUUGGGHHH!"

Jim Jeffords

Born in Rutland, Jim Jeffords served Vermont as a Republican in the U.S. Senate from 1988 until May 24, 2001, when, on live national television, he announced he would leave the GOP to become an Independent. Normally not a big deal, except his shift altered the composition of the Senate: from 50-50 to 49 Republicans, 50 Democrats, and one Independent. Jeffords retired from the Senate in 2006.

Gerald Barney

Gerald Barney is Vermont's best athlete.

"Wait a minute," you say. "What about John LeClair? You do know John LeClair, right? The first native Vermonter to play for the NHL? Born in St. Albans? Graduate of Bellows Free Academy? Played for the University of Vermont, the Montreal Canadiens, and the Philadelphia Flyers?"

Yes, I know about John LeClair, and I won't take anything away from him. But to me? Gerald Barney, of Swanton, is and always will be Vermont's best athlete.

Jerry Barney is to running what Grandpa Thompson is to garage sale-ing—machine, master, mentor. "M" cubed.

In June 2008, Jerry became one of three Mt. Washington racers to simultaneously hold two course records. For those of you unfamiliar, the grueling Mt. Washington Road Race is a 7.6-mile course that rises 4,650 vertical feet from start to finish, at the New Hampshire mountain peak. In other words—it's uphill to the death.

Jerry broke his first Mt. Washington record in his age group in 1999. He was sixty-five. When he broke his second record? In a separate age group?

He was seventy-five.

Jerry did not start running until he was forty-three years old. His runner's resumé lists more than 600 races, 28 marathons (four in Boston), 49 half-marathons, and a 50-mile race in Essex Center, Vermont—in 1980, as he kissed fifty himself.

His advice for runner's success?

"Get out the door. And stick with it."

When Jerry says that to you, you wonder if he's talking about running anymore.

Now, for some influential Vermonters . . .

George Aiken

Aiken was Vermont's Republican governor from 1937 to 1941 and the state's U.S. senator from 1941 to 1975. When he retired, he was the Senate's senior member. As governor, Aiken shattered the monopolies of many major industries, including banks, railroads, and marble and granite companies. He also encouraged co-ops for struggling farmers.

Deane C. Davis

He was a Republican governor from 1969 to 1973 and a delegate to the 1948 Republican National Convention. Before becoming governor, he worked as a lawyer, county prosecutor, superior court judge, and president of National Life Insurance Co. After he retired, he published two books of humorous stories about his experiences as a country lawyer. Davis also oversaw the enactment of Act 250.

Perry Merrill

Mr. Merrill—often called the father of Vermont skiing—established the state's vast forests and parks system.

Some other recognizable Vermont names (with natives noted)

- Henry Wells, founder of Wells Fargo and Co. Vermonter!
- Stephen A. Douglas, politician famous for debates with Abraham Lincoln. Vermonter!
- Joseph Citro, author and folklorist. Vermonter!
- Chris Bohjalian, author, *Midwives* and many more
- Jody Williams, 1997 Nobel Peace Prize winner for her work to ban land mines. Vermonter!
- Bernie Sanders, self-described "democratic socialist," U.S. senator, and former House member
- Rusty De Wees, actor, writer, and comedian best known for his backwoods Vermont character, The Logger. NOT a Vermonter, contrary to popular belief. Born in Philadelphia, PA, raised in Stowe, which is also questionable to some Vermonters.
- Tim Kavanagh, comedian, writer, actor, and former host of *Late Night Saturday*, a locally produced, Letterman-esque TV show. Vermonter!
- John Deere; yes, that John Deere. Vermonter!
- Dorothy Canfield Fisher, author and social activist
- Rudy Vallee, 1930s band leader, vocalist, radio star. Vermonter!
- William H. Macy, actor
- Michael J. Fox, actor
- David Mamet, writer
- Frank Miller, comic book artist, writer
- Aleksandr Isayevich Solzhenitsyn, author, activist
- Tantoo Cardinal, actress
- Jay Craven, filmmaker
- Billy Kidd, skier. Vermonter!
- Patty Sheehan, golfer. Vermonter!
- Bob Keeshan, aka Captain Kangaroo, the longest-running character in TV history, retired to Norwich, VT

Consuelo Northrop Bailey

A Republican who served as the nation's first female lieutenant governor, from 1955 to 1959.

The Pigman of Devil's Washbowl

Erica Goodman probably described him best in a 2004 Middlebury College newspaper story:

> In 1971, a farmer in Northfield (in an area known as Devil's Washbowl) went to investigate some strange noises coming from his backyard one night. He turned on his outside light and peered out the kitchen window, expecting to see a raccoon or plump squirrel sifting through his garbage. Instead he met the gaze of a man-sized figure lurking along the edges of the yellow light. His body was covered in white hair and he had the facial features of a pig. A few seconds later, the being darted back into the shadows.
>
> A few days passed before the Pigman was spotted again, this time by a group of students outside of the high school during a dance. Reports are vague as to who ran away faster—the students or the creature—but both quickly left the scene. Since these initial sightings, the Pigman has become a sort of "rural legend" in Northfield, and more than one nighttime traveler has claimed he encountered the Pigman while driving his car along a deserted country road, the hairy white beast narrowly missing the front end of the vehicle.

You ask me, "Why is this so-called Pigman an influential Vermonter?"

I ask you, "Why is he not?"

7

Vermont Seasons

Vermont has no NFL, MLB, NBA, WNBA, MLS, or NHL
teams. When it comes to professional sports, Vermonters are
SOL. Other seasons provide our fun.

We've all heard the Jeezum Crow–type jokes about
Vermont's four seasons: skiing, mud, construction, and foliage
(or various derivatives of the four). Vermont has a continental,
moist climate, with warm, humid summers and cold winters,
which are colder at higher elevations. Spring is followed by a
generally mild summer, with sweltering Augusts. Autumn is no
fun for the color-blind. (The TRUE color-blind, not
Independent voters.)

Those of us in Vermont base our seasons on the outdoor
activities that lend themselves to each—and you visitors
should, too, if you're smart. Leaf-peeping is no fun in January,
say, nor is that month practical for taking a dip in one of our
wonderful swimming holes. July is pretty rough sledding for
you skiers, and, well, you get the gist.

I think of Vermont's winters, springs, summers, and
autumns as snow, cigar, sandal, and stick, respectively.

Snow season

I hate winter, especially snow. Always have. Always will. I
would make a terrible Eskimo. The only good things winter has

Top five snowfalls recorded in Burlington:

103.4 inches (2007–08)
96.9 inches (1970–71)
81.7 inches (1965–66)
78.6 inches (1946–47)
75.7 inches (1969–70)

going for it are Christmas, ice fishing, and its effect on women in tight sweaters.

"But snow is beautiful," you say. Yes, it is. So are lions, and when did you last want to cuddle up with one?

Exactly.

Some Vermont parents believe their children adore snow like it was a big, purple dinosaur. Some Vermont parents are also idiots.

"But, my child tells me he loves snow," they say.

Wrong. What your child tries telling you is that he loathes snow, but he has difficulty forming sentences with his tongue frozen to your mailbox.

Vermont's average annual valley snowfall is around 100 inches (no, flatlanders, not all at once), though that amount can double or triple in the mountains. The heaviest snowfall on record in Burlington occurred in 1969, from December 25 to December 28, when 29.8 inches of the white nightmare fell to the ground. I wasn't around yet, but I do remember the Valentine's Day blizzard of 2007 that dumped anywhere from 16 to 36 inches of snow on various parts of Vermont.

The average annual high winter temperature is 53 degrees—Fahrenheit, in case you wondered. Normal high temperatures in December, January, and February are 28, 25, and 31 degrees, respectively. The normal lows during those same months are 7, 4, and 10. The lowest temperature recorded in Vermont was 50 below zero, on December 30, 1933, in

Bloomfield. That's chilly, kids. That's when we break out our toques. A toque (pronounced *tuke*) is a knitted winter cap that stretches to fit the wearer's head.

Rocky Balboa wore a toque. So did Jacques Cousteau. They wore toques with pride. Not me. Mom knew it.

"Wear your toque!" she'd yell, as I headed out the door, ready to brave winter hat-less. I'd trudge down the snow-packed sidewalk, not looking anything like Balboa or Cousteau, with what appeared to be a woolen prophylactic squeezing my head. I always risked slipping off my toque during the short walk to school, but—because she had a potato field's eyes—Mom always caught me.

Then she'd scream the French-Canadian expression that meant my funeral was imminent.

"Oh-bay, moh-teh-zee!" (I don't know what it means. I just know it scared the bejeezus outta me.)

The toque went back on my head, every time—almost.

One winter afternoon in 1985, on my way home from school, I crossed paths with the Newton brothers. Despite having the combined intelligence of Windex, the Newtons were tougher than I—not a

What to pack for snow season

If you've never seen, touched, experienced, or witnessed snow in person, on TV, or in a book, I know a good therapist. Otherwise, here are some items you should pack if you plan on visiting the Green Mountains when they're white:

- boots
- toque
- heavy coat
- gloves or mittens
- scarf
- long underwear
- small shovel (because you never know when a snowbank will reach out and swallow your car)
- Oh, yeah, and an extra toque. For when the Newtons steal yours.

difficult task. That day, they teased me about my toque, and then tossed me into a Sears Tower–high snowbank. They laughed, the way Windex would laugh. I crawled out of the cold, ivory drift and noticed a Volkswagen Jetta approaching us. It was Dad.

"You guys are in for it now!" I warned, trying to flag down Dad with my snow-covered arms. As he drove closer, I pictured him teaching the Newton brothers a thing or two about how to really throw someone in a snowbank—vengeance for toque-wearers everywhere.

"Yer gonna be sooo sorry!" I yelled. "Yer gonna . . . "

. . . *vvvrrrRRROOOooommmm* . . .

Dad. Drove. Right. By. Never even slowed down. I got a trip back to the snowbank. The Newtons got my toque. I walked home at the pace of a Florida election recount, knowing exactly what to expect: "Oh-bay, moh-teh-zee!" It was not until three hours later, when Dad returned home from work, that Mom believed my tale about the Windex-brained Newtons, the huge snowbank, and the Jetta that wouldn't stop.

Today, I still cringe at the thought of snow, but I've warmed up to wearing toques.

Mud season

My personal rite of early spring always happens during our first 45- or 50-degree night, when there are still ice-fishing shanties on Lake Champlain, and skiers still have weeks to go before putting away their gear for the season. This is when the fever kicks in. Many Vermont residents start their lawn mowers, break out their shorts and flip-flops, and stroll around bare-chested. The next day, they're shoveling snow.

One warm spring day, in the middle of mud season, Eli and Nancy are sitting out on their front porch, when Nancy looks out toward the road and says, "Eli? Ain't that a hat movin' out they-ah?"

Eli squints. "Yut. Looks like Arty McGinn's hat."

They sit and watch the hat, until Nancy says, "Eli? You don't s'pose he lost that hat in this wind, do ya?"

Eli shouts out toward the road. "Arty! You they-ah?!"

A hand rises out of the mud and tips the hat. "Mornin', Eli. Mornin', Nancy."

"You need any help, they-ah, Arty?"

"Nope, nope, nope. I'm all set. The horse knows the way."

Me? I hop in my car on that balmy night, drive to St. Albans Bay, and have a cigar on the pier, while listening to the ice shift and melt. (Yes, on warm, clear nights, you can actually hear ice melt on Lake Champlain.)

Put simply, spring in Vermont is weird. Strange. It starts when it wants and ends when it wants and ever since the global warming debate began, it hardly seems to start and end at all. Spring in Vermont is the rope in winter's and summer's annual tug-of-war. And there, underneath it all, is mud.

Mud season exists, amigos. It's real. And some Vermonters love it.

"I've lived in Vermont most of my life, and mud season is one of the best times of the year," Liz Hurd told www.scenes ofvermont.com, a Web site that is all Vermont, all the time. "When we were younger, mud season was the time of year when the sandbox would overflow and you would come inside every evening covered with mud. Now that I am in North Country Union High School, mud season is the time when everyone piles into someone's car after school, and we struggle

What to pack for mud season

- extra car, for when yours gets stuck on any given road
- hip waders (see above)
- light jacket, to fend off the wind and rain
- rod and reel, if you're interested
- and, of course, a .357 magnum—because you never know when some gangsta guppie might hop outta the water and tryta bust a cap in yo ass. (Please refer to the spring activities section of the next chapter.)

to make it down the old dirt roads. Many times we have to get out and push, allowing ourselves to be covered from head to toe with mud. All true Vermonters love mud season!"

For a 1982 *Time* magazine piece on Vermont's mud season, Montpelier resident Nona Estrin said, "We've finished watching the snow melt, and we are about to begin watching the mud dry. Both are bona fide full-time activities. You may have a full-time job, but watching spring come is the romance in your life."

And as we all know, romance equals tug-of-war.

Sandal season

You have to experience a Vermont summer to actually understand how great this season is. The normal temperatures are between the high 70s and the low 80s, plenty of days that my Uncle Turk calls "golden days," those with cloudless blue sky and a warm, soothing sun. And, I swear, those Green Mountains? They get even greener.

After the long, snowy winter, after the long, muddy spring, summer is a throw-open-the-windows-and-run-around-barefoot celebration from June through August throughout the state. I don't go barefoot, though. I wear sandals. Well, there was that one summer day I went barefoot, and the bare didn't stop there.

Summer 2008 was wet in Vermont—so rainy, that our umbrellas carried umbrellas. So when Mommy Nature gifted us a particularly beautiful Saturday, my impulsivity bone kicked in. It was so fantastic, in fact, that as I sat behind my condo with a friend, soaking up the sun, my body said, "You know what, boss? Let's ditch this bathin' suit."

Shoomp!

Down it went.

"Leon?" my friend asked. "What if your neighbor turns the corner and sees you like that?"

(I should mention this friend had different parts than me. We'll call her "Fran.")

"Good point," I said. "I just happen to know another place we can go."

She wasn't surprised.

Around 1997, shortly after I started writing for the *St. Albans Messenger*, a daily newspaper tucked in northwestern Vermont, I wrote a feature story about Maple Glen Inc., a members-only nudist campground hidden on a dirt road in Sheldon, just past the elementary school, where, naturally, a nudist campground belongs.

Fran was into checking out Maple Glen, so we logged onto its Web site to research their guest rates. Soon, she said, "Hey, let's pack a lunch!" So we did.

We pulled up to the gate, punched in the secret code we obtained over the phone before we left, and were greeted by one of Maple Glen's board directors. He drove a golf cart, and yes, of course he was nude—what did you think?

I rode shotgun. Fran sat in the back. Not on accident.

He gave us a quick tour. Maple Glen surpassed our expectations. There is an in-ground pool with an adjacent hot tub, a spacious clubhouse, a playground (you know . . . for the kids), RV and tent lots, rentable cabins, a volleyball court, and horseshoe pits, which gave new meaning to the term "ringer."

What to pack for sandal season

- sunscreen
- shorts
- T-shirts
- jeans and sweatshirt, for bonfires at night
- sandals
- beach shoes, if you're swimming in anything besides a pool
- sunscreen
- extra arms, for swatting mosquitoes and blackflies
- small bills, for state park fees and cold creemees

"What do you think?" our tan-line-less tour guide asked. "Would you like to stay for the day?"

"Absolutely," Fran said.

We disrobed at my car, left our belongings in it—unlocked, because Maple Glen has that vibe—and started down toward the clubhouse to rinse off in the shower before we hopped in the pool. Soon, I got over the fact that I was naked. It felt normal. I felt free. Fran and I swam, ate our lunch, and talked about our everyday lives with everyone else. We even went for a nice walk—all in our Happy Birthday attire.

I'll visit Maple Glen again. Actually, Vermont is full of activities and sites for nudists. Find them at: www.virtualvermonter.com/almanac/vermont_nudism.htm.

Want a companion? Look me up.

Stick season

I cannot accurately describe a Vermont autumn without including the primary activity therein. Of course, I speak of leaf-peeping.

In the fall, thousands and thousands of people converge upon Vermont for the myriad reds, yellows, and oranges that gloriously fill our trees before they all fall off. When they do, the trees are just holding up a bunch of sticks; hence, my name for the season.

Vermont's tourist industry hotly anticipates fall, because the dazzling foliage is a revenue-generating draw for the state.

In other words, flatlanders come here to watch leaves die.

Morbid, ain't it?

My all-time favorite fall foliage tree looks like a candy apple sticking out of the ground, on Route 5 in the Northeast Kingdom between Lyndonville and St. Johnsbury. Where can you see trees like that? Go to www.foliage-vermont.com.

Tourism officials have told me that flatlanders sometimes call and ask when foliage season starts. Then these same officials all laugh until their coffee comes out of their noses.

That's because foliage season is not a timed event. Our trees do not synchronize their watches, mark their calendars, and all agree on when they should stand naked and open along our paved and dirt roadsides, so that people with white license plates can take their picture and maybe even get a covered bridge in the shot, too.

Typically, Vermont's foliage season begins in the north and at high elevations before working its way south to lower elevations. All this beauty usually begins in early to mid-September and extends through mid-October, or until the trees say,

What to pack for stick season

- camera
- batteries for said camera
- map
- camera
- light jacket and hat
- comfy walking shoes
- camera
- something with which to bury any backseat drivers who won't take the wheel but will tell you what to do with it
- camera
- aaaaaand, a camera.

Also—WATCH THE ROAD! No one likes a head-on crash with a leaf-peeper.

"Show's over, folks. You can all go home. Buh-bye."

Many people consider fall Vermont's prettiest season, but it can also be its ugliest and least predictable, weatherwise. Depending on the day, time, wind direction, and various other factors—including atmospheric pressure and whether Mother Nature could obtain a permit for a surprise, early-October snowstorm— fall daytime temperatures in Vermont can range from the upper high 30s to high 60s, perhaps even warmer. Or colder. This is Vermont. Take your pick.

Average precipitation in Vermont during the fall is any- where from about two to three inches. It rains. It snows. Sometimes together.

In Vermont, we also have "Indian summer," which is a warm- ing trend of dry, moderate weather that lasts for several days.

Note: It is only a true Indian summer if it occurs after the first frost. All other Indian summers are just posers.

8

How to Enjoy Our Four Seasons

Snow-season activities

Skiing

For years, I equated skiing with NASCAR. To me, spending money to speed down an icy, snowy mountain with sticks on your feet takes as much intelligence as believing a constant left-hand turn is a sport.

Then I met Sara Jane Luneau, a Swanton girl and a self-described "ski chick," who first skied when she was three years old. She clarified things for me.

"I have vivid memories of my mother pulling me up the hill in front of our house," says Sara. "She wanted me to be able to feel the skis under my feet, and the skill of being able to pull myself back up from a fall was a plus. Although, I know that nine times out of ten, my mother was right there to pick me up."

Moms are good like that.

Sara is from a skiing clan. Her uncle Ellsworth passed on his children's equipment to her brothers, and then it became hers. Sara took her first non-mother ski lesson at age six. Her family lived forty-five minutes from Jay Peak and spent weekends on the mountain. When Sara was twelve, her mother took a job at Smugglers' Notch.

"We had wonderful perks of swimming in the pool and staying in condominiums the night of a storm," Sara recalled. "My mother perpetuated our love for skiing, because she called her own snow days. Once, the bus couldn't make it up our dirt road, so instead of bringing me and my three brothers to school, she said, 'If you can get dressed and load the car with your ski gear in fifteen minutes, we'll go skiing and not to school.' My mother taught us that fresh snow was something to relish, not detest, and a snow day was a 'powder day.' "

Sara was absent from high school thirty-nine days—thirty-five of them spent on skis. Plus weekends. Later, while living in Colorado, she skied more than one hundred days a year. Now, she averages about thirty-five days a season and has the stories to prove it. Sara has witnessed a friend set off a small avalanche; taken a slow-motion, backwards fall off the side of a trail and hit her head on a tree (a concussion ensued); and—as a child—was stuck on a tram for ninety minutes.

Ski slopes are like mini-cities, according to Sara. "Ski bums" likely have duct tape on their poles and make runs with backpacks. Canadian skiers wear fanny packs. New Jersey skiers dress in neon colors or in jackets emblazoned with their favorite football team's logo (GO GIANTS!).

Sara also was kind enough to define the different types of snow that skiers enjoy:

Powder: In Vermont, it's defined as any form of white flakes that accumulate two inches or more and make for ideal skiing. "Skiers live for powder days," Sara said. "They cause people to wake early, drive in blizzards, stand in line, wait for the lifts to open, and yell while skiing. 'Yeee-haaaw!' 'Ohhh, yeaaahhh!' There is no such thing as friends on powder days."

Packed powder: Conditions on the day after powder.

Frozen granular: Snow that has "death cookies," otherwise known as ice chunks, scattered throughout the trail. "Frozen granular is not quite snow, but it isn't ice, either," Sara said. (Also comes in "loose granular.")

Ice: Caused mostly by rainstorms, it's either blue or clear, so that you can see rocks underneath it. Rainy conditions can also result in a coat of ice covering your goggles. "We refer to this as 'skiing by Braille,' " Sara said.

Corn: When the temperatures soar during spring conditions and the snow softens, you're skiing on corn. " 'Cream corn' is the ultimate corn and is effortless skiing, because your skis slither through the snow," Sara explained. "It is like skiing on soft cream cheese."

True skiers have esoteric terms for other skiers: SPORE: Stupid Person on Rental Equipment
   Poser: Someone who has the best equipment and top-of-the-line clothing, who skis in highly visible areas (such as under the chairlift), and who can't really ski. At all.
   PSIA: "Asshole in stretch pants" spelled backwards.
   Poachers: People who ski under the "keep out" rope, or on closed trails.

Sara has skied just about every mountain in Vermont—Jay Peak, Smugglers' Notch, Stowe, Mad River Glen. Name it, and she's probably flown down it. She also showers kudos on the state's smaller, lesser-known hills, such as Bromley Mountain in southern Vermont, Hard'ack in St. Albans Town, and Cochran's, a Richmond ski area started by Mickey and Ginny Cochran, whose children were medal-winning Olympic and world-class skiers.

"Our mountains offer terrain for various ski abilities, while offering beautiful mountain vistas," Sara said, in a tone that makes me wonder if she's taking kickbacks from the Vermont Ski Areas

Association. "Our Vermont mountains create an indomitable ski spirit among Vermont skiers."

At which point, I told Sara I don't ski.

Pregnant pause.

"I think that any Vermonter who doesn't ski is missing out on what it is to be a true Vermonter," she said. "Skiing makes winter tolerable, even if it is thirty below zero. I'm not sure I would live in Vermont, if I didn't ski."

Hmmmm.

The ski areas

Smugglers' Notch is the first thing that crosses Sara's brain when she hears the words "Vermont ski area." It's near Stowe.

"A couple of things come to mind," she said. "It's family fun. But they have the most antiquated ski lifts. Slow. And the longest lines. But Smugglers' Notch is known for producing the hardy skiers."

"Do you see a lot of out-of-staters?"

"Families of them."

Killington, in central Vermont just east of Rutland, is dominated by New Yorkers, Sara said. "As a matter of fact, it's probably the only ski area in Vermont where a Yankees cap is preferred over a Red Sox cap. They pride themselves on opening really early—before there's even snow in the valley—and being the last one to close. Killington is also known for its bumps."

That's "moguls" for all you non-skiers like me.

"I think you have to say that Stowe is the ski capital of the East," Sara advised me. "It's been their slogan for years now. They produce Olympic racers there."

Sara also had some words of advice for you flatlanders who've never skied here.

"Mad River Glen? No snowboarders allowed. And it's owned by shareholders, who are typically season passholders. And it has a single chair lift.

"But Mad River Glen has the most challenging terrain, and that's great. They do the least amount of snowmaking and trail grooming, so it's all about Mother Nature and ski ability."

After hearing Sara talk so passionately about skiing, I thought a run down a mountain might be in my future.

Don't think I'll start watching NASCAR, though.

(Go to www.skivermont.com/alpine for a list of the state's ski areas.)

Mt. Mansfield Stone Hut

The closest I ever came to skiing (minus skis, boots, goggles, and actually going up and down a mountain in winter) was in January 2007, when, for a little getaway, my friends Stina and Jason reserved the Mt. Mansfield Stone Hut—elevation 3,600 feet, no electricity, no running water, no problem. Or . . . so I thought. A group of us agreed to make the trip.

As you might have surmised, I'm not very outdoorsy. I mean, I know where the outdoors is. I've been there. And enjoyed it. During warm-weather months, I visit it frequently, with a cigar in hand. But you won't find me hosting my own show on Animal Planet anytime soon.

Lucky for me—Mr. Which Way to My Feet?—there was no compass necessary en route to the Hut. It was all up, all the time. Almost three miles, yet it felt like 350 miles, and the trek took about three hours, mostly because it was hot, at least for January in Vermont—hot in an Al Gore, *Inconvenient Truth* kinda way.

The first night, all eleven of us became acquainted by lanterns and headlamps over burritos and Johnny Cash, courtesy of iPod. We also read the rules and associated fines posted in the hut:

- Mattress damage (or use as sleds)—$100
- Graffiti —$7.50 per square inch

(and my favorite . . .)
- Bodily fluids outside the hut—$50

If any of us felt fifty bucks coming on, we walked a short distance to The Octagon, a restaurant near a ski lift. We had a key for bathroom use after hours there. The key was handy. Which I learned. The hard way.

Next day, it rained. Hard. All day, pretty much. We even got a mountaintop, wintertime thunderstorm. Eventually, though, the skies cleared, and some of us thought, Wow, wouldn't it be great to catch the sunset on the tip of Mt. Mansfield's nose?

Beforehand, I took a few minutes to unload my burritos at The Octagon and discovered the only place with a cell phone signal—so I could call my daughter—was a men's-room stall. Great time to multitask. Or so I thought.

Unbeknownst to me, The Octagon closes at 3:40 p.m. so the employees can catch the ski lift down before it stops at 4 o'clock. My advice? Unload your burritos by 3. And stay off the phone.

Luckily, one of the ski lift operators heard me kicking The Octagon door. He retrieved the key from the Hut and rescued me, leaving everyone else to have a good laugh at my expense.

Hard to believe, I know.

I highly recommend the Mt. Mansfield Stone Hut www.vtstateparks.com/htm/stonehut.cfm.

Cross-country, snowshoeing, snowmobiling

Maybe you like ice and snow, but you're more the sea-level type. You have three options in Vermont: cross-country skiing, snowshoeing, and what I like to call "redneck chariot racing"— snowmobiling.

I suppose that for ski bums, cross-country skiing is considered "skiing light," because you're not shooting down a mountain with nothing but a helmet protecting your thoughts-holder.

Actually, cross-country skiing originated in prehistoric times, when Neanderthals in Fennoscandian countries, such as Norway and Sweden, moved and hunted by propelling themselves across the snow with wooden planks secured to their feet. Today, Vermont has 885 miles of well-groomed, cross-country skiing trails at thirty Nordic resorts. Go to www.skivermont.com.

And then there's snowshoeing—the act of distributing your weight over the snow so that you don't sink completely. This is called "flotation."

I haven't been snowshoeing, either, but snowshoeing has existed in the Green Mountains for more than two centuries, and was once considered a mode of New England transportation. Now, non-skiers from all over view Vermont as a snowshoeing destination.

For a list of snowshoeing sites in Vermont and tour operators, go to www.vtliving.com.

Maybe you like your winter fun to be loud and fast and full of gas. Well, there's always a snowmobile. I've been on a snowmobile once, which doesn't make me ripe for a membership to the Vermont Association of Snow Travelers (www.vtvast.org).

Ice fishing

Me? I'm more the ice-fishing type.

Ice fishing is just what it says: fishing through a hole in the ice, put there, of course, by aliens. Vermont is part of what is known as the "Ice Belt," which also includes Minnesota, North Dakota, South Dakota, Wisconsin, Montana, Colorado, Wyoming, Nebraska, Idaho, Iowa, Illinois, Indiana, Michigan, Ohio, New York, Pennsylvania, Maine, and New Hampshire.

Ice-fishing season starts as early as Thanksgiving in some Midwestern states and as late as Christmas for East Coast states, including Maine. In Vermont, if there's frost on a pumpkin, there's some idiot walking across a thin coat of ice, praying to Dale Earnhardt that he doesn't fall through and miss his chances at catching an abundance of perch.

But why walk when you can drive? And people do. Typically, there should be at least four inches of new, clear ice if you want to walk out and fish. Five inches are necessary for snowmobiles and ATVs, and eight to twelve inches are good for cars and other larger vehicles.

Fishermen are good at judging ice depth without measuring it, because all they have to do is equate it with the thickness of their skulls.

The biggest benefit to ice fishing is that it's the one winter sport that doesn't require expensive equipment, a pass, or a ride on a chairlift next to some Jersey-ite named Mo. All you need to ice-fish is a fishing license.

Two things, though: 1) Ice fishing is risky. 2) Ice fishermen are loco. Combine the two like I did on my last ice-fishing excursion, and the trip is as fun as the fire down below.

I drove to my friend Brian's house on a white, bright, Vermont-postcard Saturday, just after downing a leftover linguini breakfast. "Nut," which I call Brian because he is one, drove to the store for necessary supplies: two bags of tortilla chips, two jars of salsa (one hot, one mild), and two cases of beer.

What can I say? Ice fishing spurs an insatiable thirst.

Some ice fishermen refuse to drive on the ice. Not Nut. He hit the hard water and made way for Don's Hideaway, a shanty owned by his stepfather. Don's Hideaway is beyond shanty—a ten-by-sixteen-foot Graceland on ice with two beds, chairs, a card table, a stove, a propane heater, and a portable toilet, which I assume goes unused, considering the ice surrounding Don's Hideaway glows like a glass of lemonade.

Nut, our bud Butch, and I each fished with a line in the water. Three men. Three lines. Not a bite. Then Uncle Turk arrived with his two pals, Dan and a case of beer.

"You guys can't fish," Turk said. "Move the line like this." He squatted over a nonexistent hole and milked an invisible cow. "Want me to show ya how to catch some fish?"

"You crazy fool," Nut said. "We've been here forty minutes and ain't had a bite. You won't catch nothin'."

I handed Turk my line. He jiggled it furiously, let it sit, and jiggled it again. Suddenly, he snapped it back, while Nut and I exchanged glances and smiled. Turk caught that day's only perch in 33.4 seconds.

"I'm not catchin' another one 'til you guys do," he said.

Butch threw Turk's gilled miracle back into the hole and proclaimed, "That ain't a fish. The minnow's are bigger'n 'at thing."

The absence of a radio in the shanty made Butch our designated entertainment. He is a six-foot, five-inch, 350-pound, tobacco-spitting mountain of profanity. Dan is six feet, 290 pounds. After Don arrived with a fresh twelve-pack (and to see if his hideaway was still standing, I'm sure), Dan and Butch decided to play Pass the Minnow—with their mouths.

No, no, no . . . it gets worse.

After an unruly, booze-soaked night nearby at an American Legion hall, I opened my eyes Sunday morning and there, snuggled beside me, was Dan. Thank God I didn't have minnow breath.

(For more, go to www.vtliving.com.)

Mud-season activities

Fishing

In late mud season, er, late spring, fishing remains popular—and stays that way throughout the year, come to think of it—mainly because the water is still high. It's quite a sight, watching gobs of fishermen with full coolers build small fires at the high-water marks along St. Albans Bay, and casting their lines . . .

. . . into the road.

Like I said, the water gets high during the spring thaw.

Every year, Lake Champlain International gives hundreds of fishermen the chance to win big prizes. Lake Champlain International, Inc., is a federally recognized 501(c)(3) non-profit corporation, which, in Vermont, means it is run mostly by transplants. The LCI says its mission is "conservation, restoration and revitalization of Lake Champlain and the Lake Champlain watershed." The LCI's biggest fund-raiser is its Father's Day Derby, where, every year, fathers and sons from all over the country do their part to restore and revitalize Lake Champlain by drinking beer and yanking our fish from their natural habitat.

Good fishermen cast lines at the LCI. Bad fishermen just end up writing books like this.

(For more information on the LCI Father's Day Derby, go to www.lciderby.com.)

Our lakes and rivers are packed with all sorts of scaled critters in all shapes and sizes, from brook trout, bass, and bullpout to walleye, sturgeon, and northern pike. Want to take a peek at the state's fishing records? Go to www.statefishingrecords.com/vermont.htm. Want to know where to catch your own? Then check out www.aa-fishing.com/vt/vermont-map.html. There, you will see where to catch panfish, salmon, and more. The site lists hotels and restaurants, and posts various articles and blogs about fishing.

One of the state's more unique and—if we're going to be honest—stupid mud-season pastimes also surrounds fishing, except you don't need bait, boats, or tackle boxes.

Only bullets.

Shooting fish is legal in Vermont, although the state fish and wildlife folks don't condone it, because—as you might recall from high school physics—bullets ricochet across water. Also, the state likes to keep this one a little on the down-low, because, well, what would the tourists think if they drove by a northwestern shore of Lake Champlain in late April and saw a redneck aimin' his huntin' rifle over the water.

"Nine-one-one. What's your emergency?"

"My Gawd, my gawd! It's just terrible! I'm driving past the lake, visiting from Connecticut, and there's a man pointing a gun over the water! I think he's going to kill someone! If he hasn't already!"

"Okay, ma'am. Calm down. Now, did you get a good look at this individual?"

"Yes! Yes! He's still here! Send someone now!"

"Okay, now, ma'am? I just need you to stay with me and answer a question for me. Okay?"

"Okay."

"Can you pull over and lemme know if he fires at a northern or a walleye? Cuz I wuz thinkin' of headin' down there myself later. And if there's nothin' worth firin' at, I might just go home and mow the lawn."

Tapping

Meanwhile in the spring, in order to convey the image that Vermont-made syrup actually comes from maple trees and not from bottles shaped like bandana-ed women, producers engage in a spring activity known as "tapping trees." This is done to collect the sap that ostensibly becomes the syrup and is done in one of three ways:

- hanging metal buckets and spouts off the trees;
- devising a system of clear, plastic tubing that runs the sap from the trees to the sugarhouse;
- actually tapping a tree on its trunk and begging.

Incidentally, the world's leading manufacturer of maple sugaring equipment, Leader Evaporator, is based in Swanton.

You can see what I mean by visiting some sugarhouses that open their doors to tourists and the like. Go to: www.vermont maple.org.

Sandal-season activities

Camping

I related my pleasant nudist camp experience in the previous chapter, but there are more conventional campgrounds in

Vermont, where, indeed, clothing is required, and where I, as a child with my family, spent many a summer week or weekend. I have vivid memories of pumping several dollars' worth of quarters into a hungry Galaga machine at the Homestead Campgrounds in Georgia, just south of St. Albans. (That was my idea of camping. I told you I was an inside kid.) Then there were the summers we'd ward off armies of raccoons who raided the coolers outside our lean-tos at Lake Carmi State Park in Franklin.

My directionally challenged (but only in Vermont) friend Kathy, from a previous chapter, once accepted a request to help on a Girl Scout camping trip to Camel's Hump State Park, near Richmond. The ten scouts, ages seven and eight, had a spaghetti dinner before they gathered 'round the campfire for s'mores, skits, and, songs. At bedtime, the girls unrolled their sleeping bags inside a three-sided, wooden lean-to.

Kathy was soon asleep, too, but awoke when she heard a gurgling noise emerge from the sleeping bag next to her. As a parent, she quickly pegged the sound as a seven-year-old's stomach emptying its spaghetti and s'mores into a sleeping bag. Kathy scooped up the sleeping bag—with the child inside— and lugged it out of the lean-to. She took the girl out, cleaned her off, and brought her to the nurse.

When Kathy returned to the lean-to, everyone else was asleep, but there were noises coming from the nauseated girl's sleeping bag. Kathy shined her flashlight toward the bag and saw five ginormous raccoons cleaning it out.

One major must for camping in Vermont: raccoon repellent. Keep the spaghetti at home.

On its Web site, www.vtstateparks.com, the Vermont State Park system lists pictures, campground maps, amenities, rates, area attractions, weather, and more. The state suggests you make reservations first, and fees vary, depending on whether you want to stay for the day or season, go boating, have a picnic, or camp overnight in a cabin or cottage. (Say that ten times fast. I dare ya.)

Most importantly, if you like a good campfire, do not—I repeat, do not—bring wood from outside Vermont, because it could be infected with non-native, invasive species. Transplants are bad enough. We don't need multi-legged flatlanders deciding they love it here and thinking they should stay, too.

Hiking

Adventurous campers and hikers from all over the world journey to Vermont for the Long Trail, the oldest long-distance trail in the U.S. Built by the Green Mountain Club from 1910 to 1930, the Long Trail stretches 272 miles from the Massachusetts border to North Troy, on the cusp of Canada. The Long Trail inspired the Appalachian Trail, which coincides with it for 100 miles in the southern third of Vermont.

The Long Trail has 175 miles of side trails and about seventy primitive shelters. Day hikers, weekend overnighters, and extended-stay backpackers hit the Long Trail during all times of the year, but mainly in the summer.

Completing the Long Trail is an ambitious goal for many serious hikers. Those who try and succeed keep journals filled with written memories of their experiences. My friend Peter let me borrow his journal from his Long Trail trek, which transpired from 1999 to 2008. (Nobody says you have to complete the trail in one fell swoop.) During that time, Peter, a hospital administrator, turned fifty, watched two daughters graduate from high school, and underwent knee surgery.

"The trail mirrors your life," Peter says. "Whether you're going through work or kids or birthdays, you fit in the Long Trail as you can. And it's a culture. It's a rare exception to run into an asshole up there."

Peter spent his days on the Long Trail with his friends Larry (a probate judge), Howard (a district court judge), and Bruce (who, apparently, isn't the best judge of character, given the company he keeps while hiking). Along the way, they woke to a moose outside their tent, saw countless bear prints, went a quarter-mile in three hours during a powerful windstorm, and camped on an old railroad bed.

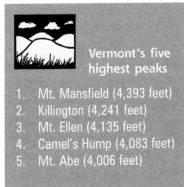

Vermont's five highest peaks

1. Mt. Mansfield (4,393 feet)
2. Killington (4,241 feet)
3. Mt. Ellen (4,135 feet)
4. Camel's Hump (4,083 feet)
5. Mt. Abe (4,006 feet)

Highlights included: a weeklong, fifty-five- to sixty-mile trek from Stratton to Chittenden; a twelve-mile day hike through Devil's Gulch; and Larry's chicken and beef stew.

Here are some excerpts from Peter's journal:

July 1999: Larry, Bruce, Howard and myself left for a day hike . . . Beautiful day for a walk . . . Very tough downhill and the trail was in good shape. . . . A great day.

Sept. 18, 1999: Just learned from Larry and Howard that this sucker is 272 miles long, not 2.7 miles, as I originally thought. Ska-roo this! I'm outta here.

Sept. 19, 1999: Back at it. Wife found out how much I spent on all this hiking and camping gear and threatened to bruise precious parts of my anatomy if I didn't finish this trip . . . Up early, and everything is achy. Time to eat and move along. Grrr . . .

Peter said the Long Trail's best offering—maybe second to the awesome views from Jay Peak and Mt. Mansfield—is that it's tailored for people at all levels of hiking. Take, for example, my friend Kelley. One weekend, when her clan was gathered at her grandmother's house, they decided to take a short hike on the Long Trail. Kelley went with her two sisters, her aunt and uncle, their three children, and her parents. Her father was on crutches.

About halfway through their planned course, they passed another pair of Long Trailers.

"The rest of the way shouldn't be a problem for most of you," one of them said, "but the gentleman on crutches might have a hard time."

Kelley's father stayed ahead of everyone.

"We did wind up giving up and going home, but not due to my dad," Kelley said. "It was due to the fact that it was getting dark, and we had no camping supplies."

But they can say they spent time on the Long Trail.

(For more information on the Long Trail, visit www.green mountainclub.org.)

Vermont Living Internet magazine (www.vtliving.com) has a complete list of other hiking trails that are listed regionally. The site also lists several attributes of each trail, including directions, total distance, average hiking time, vertical rise, and ratings— which range from "Easy" and "Moderate" to "Strenuous" and "Frickin A, I Shoulda Stayed Home and Watched the Red Sox."

Swimming holes

Just briefly, we should mention Vermont's hidden and beautiful swimming holes. You can find eighty-nine of them at: www.swimmingholes.org/vt.html. Some are listed simply by

the town in which they're in (Arlington, Bolton, Mad River);
some have unique names (Glen Lake, Hapgood Pond, The
Ledges); and some are named after anatomical parts we don't
want to know anything about (Adam's Hole, Benson's Hole,
and Buttermilk Falls—known as "Butt").

A word of advice: You might want to avoid Huntington
River Gorge in Richmond. Twenty-two people have died there
since 1950, and a Vermont State Police trooper drowned while
trying to recover a body there in the early 1990s.

Sorry to kill your buzz, but I want you safe, so you can finish this book and urge your friends to buy it, too.

Stick-season activities

Hunting

After the leaf-peeping frenzy has subsided, after the leaves
are raked, bagged, burned, or turned into scarecrow stuffing,
and the trees are displaying their bare-naked sticks, hunting
season has arrived.

Vermont's woods and forests are packed with various
species: moose, rabbits, squirrels, muskrats, woodchucks, fisher
cats, coyotes (or coy dogs), black bear, wild turkey (both in the
bottle and in the woods), fox, pheasants, deer, beaver, and that
mouse head that my friend Bridget once found lodged between
two pieces of salmon in a frozen dinner entree. Human behavior
and several other causes have put about 200 animals and plants
on the state's endangered and threatened species list. The common loon, spiny softshell turtle, sedge wren, and wild lupine
are all on the roster, and another 600 or so animals and plants

are considered rare or uncommon in Vermont, according to the Vermont Earth Institute.

Just prior to publication of this book, there was a move afoot in Vermont to map the state's vernal pools.

 About the only mammals you can't hunt in Vermont are the camels that live in a field on Route 7, in Ferrisburgh, and—if you see one—a catamount.

Catamounts are Vermont's wildcat versions of Champ. Once rampant in the state, they have become elusive. A catamount sighting in Vermont is a newsworthy event.

What should you do if you see a catamount?
1. Summon it. ("Heeere, kitty, kitty, kittyyy . . . ")
2. Stick out your hand, so it can smell you.
3. Let the fun begin.

"Vernal pool?" you wonder. "Is that another one of your relatives?"

No, but that's a great guess.

Vernal pools are the forest puddles of snowmelt that form in March and dry up during the summer. Birds, turtles, snakes, and some types of frogs might use vernal pools as restaurants and resting points, but these mini-ponds also provide crucial habitat for wood frogs, three species of salamanders, and fairy shrimp.

Vermont has different hunting seasons and regulations for differ-ent critters. Moose-hunting per-mits were first issued in 1993. Vermont is the top turkey-hunting state in New England. You can hunt bear with dogs in Vermont.

And there is no . . . ah, hell, if I listed all the rules and regula-tions here, I wouldn't have enough room to finish this book. To learn more about hunting and fishing in Vermont, and what the penalties are for jacking deer—which isn't anything like chang-ing a tire, despite how it sounds—visit www.vtfishandwildlife.com.

Deer-hunting season is probably the most popular among Vermont outdoorsmen, who unabashedly smear doe urine on their clothes to attract rut bucks. (If I had a band, I'd call it "Rut Bucks." Picture the marquee now: RUT BUCKS LIVE! ONE NIGHT ONLY!)

Duxbury's Benoit Brothers—Lanny, Shane, and Lane—are often called The First Family of Deer Hunting. With 100 years of hunting experience among them, they have collectively bagged vast amounts of gigantic bucks. Their first book, *Big Bucks the Benoit Way*, has sold more than 40,000 copies since publication in the 1990s. Their second book, *Benoit Bucks*, features a chapter on each brother and the "most common mistakes that hunters make," such as standing near Dick Cheney when his rifle's loaded.

I haven't read the Benoits' books, but I assume they don't delve deeply into the most key aspect of deer hunting: camp.

For a virtual Vermont deer camp experience at home, follow these steps:

1. Get rid of your spouse and children for two weeks.

2. Dress yourself in six layers of camouflage and a blinding orange vest.

3. Purchase twelve cases of beer (preferably a brand that rots your tongue, such as Natural Light or Milwaukee's Best). Scatter the empty cans throughout your home. Except for the occasional doughnut and spicy beef jerky strip, the brew will be your only sustenance.

4. Dim the lights, stand in a bucket of cold water, and watch *Deliverance* on constant rotation.

5. Do not bathe.

6. Leave only when the beer runs out. (If it appears as though the beer will last the full fortnight, you have botched the entire operation.)

Grandpa Thompson was the EEWC's patriarch. In late 2007, at age eighty-two, he survived a bout with colon cancer. Anyone who's tried to tell a retired railroad man that he needs his caboose examined can understand the struggle this caused. Especially when that railroad man's health was historically strong.

Ironically, the cancer didn't bother him; slowing down did. But he didn't slow too much, until the following fall. That November, Grandpa's auditory senses conked, frail from years of exposure to train engines during the day and a houseful of eight children at night. The hearing aids he wore for years surrendered. He communicated with a dry-erase board. Then came diabetes and speculation that he might face prostate cancer. Grandpa's glowing face and mood darkened. Frustration set in. He felt off track. Out of steam. Stuck in a tunnel.

Soon into deer-hunting season, my cousin Billy asked Grandpa to join him in the woods.

"I'd love to, ol' man," Grandpa said, as Grandma translated for him. "But I'm just not up to it. I don't think I could. I'm sorry."

"Okay," Billy said. "Some other time."

Three days later, Billy, his father, Turk, and their friend Eric were in the woods, trying to corner a buck.

"We need a fourth person," Eric said.

"I'll get Dad," Uncle Turk said.

"I don't think it'll work," Billy said. "I already asked him to hunt with me. I don't think he will."

"I'll give it a try," Uncle Turk said. "I'll be back."

"No," Grandpa snapped, as Uncle Turk stood in his doorway. "I can't, Turk. I can't hear. I can't hunt. I'm useless."

Uncle Turk took a breath. "Okay," he said. "I'm leaving in three minutes. You'll either be ready, or not."

Two minutes later, Grandpa emerged from his bedroom, half-dressed and disheveled, like a first-grader dressing himself for the first day of school. "Let's go."

Uncle Turk brought him to their hunting spot.

"All you gotta do is sit here," Uncle Turk said. "Maybe make some noise. Scare him toward one of us."

Turk walked away and didn't get far, before—bang! He sprinted back. As wet leaves and twigs flew from underneath his booted feet, he wondered what possessed him to bring his eighty-three-year-old father into the woods with a loaded gun.

Grandpa was still seated. "Look what I did," he said. He grinned. Widely. A three-point, 107-pound deer lay lifeless on the ground.

"He walked right toward me," Grandpa told Uncle Turk. "He looked at me, turned to his side, and stood there. So I fired."

Looked at him. Turned to its side. And waited.

Grandpa had not used his lifetime hunting license in sixteen years. That deer was a gift.

No matter what it costs, no matter where it comes from, no matter how it's wrapped or packaged or meant to be used, a gift should perform only one task for you.

Matter.

Ta-daaa! Welcome to deer camp

My last trip to deer camp was in 1997, with a band of relatives known as the East Enosburg Whitetail Club—EEWC, for short. It's pronounced "Euuuck," which is the sound a hunter makes after he eats a bowl of corn chowder that has sat on the camp stove—untouched—for twelve hours.

Next to cheap beer and poker money, beards and a blinding orange wardrobe are the two most important components at EEWC camp. Unfortunately, I have a receding face line. No beard for me. As for the glowing garments? Blinding orange is safe; I'll give it that. After all, who would kill a Hawaiian sunset because he thought it was a deer?

But why orange, of all colors? Why not a hellish red? Hunters should wear safe colors that say, "I am in the woods! I am ready for the kill! I embody danger!"

Orange says, "I am a traffic cone."

As is the case at most deer camps, plumbing at the EEWC HQ requires the hunter to dump a bucket of water down the bowl when the deed is done; that calls for a road trip. During that 1997 excursion, five of us climbed into Uncle Dick's truck—the official deer camp vehicle—and went to retrieve toilet water. On our journey to the water hole, which occurred during a snowstorm, Uncle Dick's truck fishtailed down a back road covered with ice.

"I got it!" Uncle Dick exclaimed, after the initial swerve. We knew better than that, yet he repeated the phrase after the next two jolts. His truck sped from ten to forty miles per hour in five seconds, and our travel path was about as straight as Elton John. Another passenger gave Uncle Dick some sound advice.

"Take the ditch! Take the ditch!"

Uncle Dick ignored his suggestion. The truck was about to become a rolling pin and flatten all life forms that straddled the left embankment. Suddenly, a shoulder of snow appeared miraculously. The truck straightened. So did our breathing.

"Whoa, air! I got chest pains now, air," another passenger joked. "I think I need an EKG, air."

At the water hole, Uncle Dick said, "You know, I didn't have it back air."

Thanks for the newsflash, Katie Couric.

Back then, Uncle Dick had his pilot's license and explained how pilots are trained to reassure passengers of total safety during a crisis.

"That's not reassurance," I said. "That's lying."

Which also happens at deer camp. Just so you know.

9

Places to Go

A floating bridge, a stoned gorilla, and a hole inna head

Perhaps you've heard of the Mile-High Club. If not, buy a plane ticket to anywhere, and ask your flight attendant about joining. Let me know how that works out for you.

Vermont has a "251 Club" that is totally unaffiliated with the Mile-High Club—although, wow, that would be awesome. Anyway, members of the 251 Club (www.vt251.com) try to visit all of Vermont's 251 cities and towns, and places that were towns. Those that hit all of them are "plus members."

Commentator Arthur Wallace Peach first suggested the 251 Club in a 1954 issue of *Vermont Life* magazine. The club now has many official members that meet biannually; my friend, Hannah, is one of them. Hannah, a Ryegate Corner native, made it a mission to earn her plus-member status while serving as Miss Vermont in 2000, and completed her 'round-the-state tour in six months.

To do that, I'd have to tighten a few soft spots and brush up on my talent portion of the program, unless the Miss Vermont contest appreciates earth-shattering flatulence. But I doubt it.

While I ponder this, why don't you sit back and learn a thing or twenty about some different parts of Vermont?

Our largest cities, in order, are:

Burlington

You must, must, must see Burlington, because it really is Boston's and New York's adopted gay son. We don't call it "the Queen City" for nothing.

Burlington is our state's biggest, transplant-filled city with 39,000 people, 10,000 of whom are college students. In 2006, Burlington was ranked the ninth-best American city in which to live. Its culturally vibrant downtown is on the Lake Champlain waterfront, and the Church Street Marketplace—a four-block pedestrian mall in the center of the city—is a people-watcher's dream. (Singer KT Tunstall got her start on Church Street.)

The Ethan Allen Homestead is in Burlington, along with the ECHO Lake Aquarium and Science Center. The Firehouse Center for the Visual Arts is amazing, and the Robert Hull Fleming Museum is an archaeology-lover's delight. Burlington also has a fantastic bike path and shares a professional basketball franchise, the Vermont Frost Heaves, with Barre.

Admittedly, those thirty-mile childhood trips from Swanton to Burlington with my family packed in the station wagon was a metropolitan treat for me. All those stores. All those restaurants. All those people. Good times.

To some, Burlington is the heart of Vermont.

To others, it's where Ted Bundy was born. (Really.)

Rutland

With a population that kisses 18,000, Rutland is Vermont's second-largest city. The online Urban Dictionary calls it "Rut Vegas," not endearingly. Unfortunately, Rutland's reputation as the New Jersey of Vermont started in 1894, when the nation's first polio outbreak occurred there.

What many people don't realize is that Rutland has more to offer than sprawl development on Route 7. In 2009, Rutland celebrated its fiftieth anniversary of an awesome, comic book–themed Halloween parade that was actually the setting of some comics in the early 1970s. (Rutland officials maintain the event is the oldest Halloween parade in the U.S.)

Rutland's downtown contains the Rutland Free Library, the Paramount Theater, and Merchant's Row, a restored street dating back to the mid-1800s. One hundred and eight buildings in downtown Rutland are listed on the National Register of Historic Places.

Rutland also has the 275-acre Pine Hill Park with mountain biking, hiking, and more. The Vermont State Fair is also in Rutland.

The waitress and the diner that make Rutland great

Then there's Pauline, at the Midway Diner.

During the same road trip that the Molly Stark Trail almost took my life, I spent a night in Rutland. I arrived groggy and cranky. Too much coffee. Not enough water. A four-mile run woke me and made me hungry for food and local color. I remembered the sign on Route 7 north: Midway Diner & Steakhouse. In a town filled with big-box stores, Midway's half-century-old facade is hard to miss—Graceland behind a Mobil station.

Midway makes Rutland.

My whole body exhaled when I walked inside, heard Fats Domino on the ceiling speakers, and saw the two-tone gray bar and stools up front. Cellophane-wrapped slices of pie waited to escape the glass dessert case. An overweight, mustached cook

101

peered through the plastic window in the double-swinging doors, wondering who was outside.

Pauline had light, bouffant hair and a nametag decorated with two pins: a red, polyester heart near the upper right-hand corner; and a butterfly with pearl wings on the lower left-hand corner. She's worked at Midway for thirty-nine years, twenty-seven of them on the eleven-to-seven shift. Flo, kiss her grits.

"I needed this," I muttered to Pauline, scanning the loaded menu.

"Why's that?" she asked.

"I spent most of the day surrounded by skiers. This is more my style."

"Well, honey, you just make yourself right at home."

Pauline called me "sweetie," "honey" and "dearie." The two-syllable words women throw at me aren't typically that kind.

Regulars filled Midway. Fast. Excluding a family of seven, the average customer's age was fifty-five; hence the abundance of hot, open-faced sandwiches on the menu. (Older Vermonters love hot, open-faced sandwiches. It's the gravy, baby. The gravy.)

"What's free tonight?" a regular asked Marybeth.

"Nu'in'," she said. "But you get a free bill with every meal."

Marybeth is great, but Pauline is the heart of Midway. That night, she, not Burlington, felt like the heart of Vermont.

Like any diner worth its weight in I LOVE VERMONT sugar packets, Midway serves breakfast all day. I ordered the He-Man: scrambled eggs, three pieces of French toast, ham, bacon, sausage, and Vermont maple syrup. And coffee. Again. Pauline kept it hot for me. (I tipped her better than I normally tip cows.)

"You need more coffee, dearie?" she asked.

"Only when it's convenient for you," I said.

She laughed. "Well, it's not convenient, but you're gonna get some anyway."

According to Pauline, Midway opened as a "silver diner"—an eatery in a trailer—in 1949. The new owners built Midway's current incarnation in the 1990s and moved the old structure.

"It was the stupidest thing they ever did," Pauline said. "A lot of people still talk about that old diner."

Marybeth took the money for my tab: $12 for the best meal I had all weekend. I mentioned this book. She liked the idea.

"If you want more information on this place," she said, "you should talk to Nancy. She's worked here fifty-five years, but she only works mornings, Monday through Thursday."

"Someone has worked here longer than Pauline?" I asked, shocked.

"Most of our girls have been here around thirty years," Marybeth said.

"You must have a lot of regulars."

"Sure do. That's how we survive."

South Burlington

It has the largest mall in Vermont, the University Mall, with more than seventy stores and a food court.

The largest mall in the world is the South China Mall in—you guessed it—China. It opened in 2005 and has windmills, theme parks, and 7.1 million square feet of gross lease-able area.

The University Mall has Kohl's.

South Burlington's finest treasure—and one of Vermont's—isn't in the middle of the city; it's on Interstate 89.

Reverence, a sculpture created by artist Jim Sardonis in 1989, is a pair of whale tails, made from African black granite, that stick about thirteen feet out of the ground, between exits twelve and thirteen. British metals trader David Threlkeld lived in Randolph when he commissioned *Reverence*.

Sea creatures in New England's only landlocked state.

That's Vermont for you.

Barre

Barre needs a bumper sticker that says STONED SINCE 1781.

With 9,000 people, Barre City—which operates as a separate municipality from its surrounding town, also called "Barre," because that's how we do things around here—is rich, rich, rich in granite history that started with the discovery of vast deposits at Millstone Hill, soon after the War of 1812. Barre's granite industry exploded when the railroad arrived. "Barre Gray" granite is "popular for its fine grain, even texture, and superior weather resistance, making it preferable among outdoor-sculpture artists," according to something I read on the Internet.

Barre's most aesthetic display of its granite is in Hope Cemetery, a sixty-five-acre spread with more than 10,000 ornately crafted gravestones and tombstones. It is estimated that one-third of all memorials in the U.S. come from Barre.

St. Albans City

Every April, St. Albans' population of 10,000 easily quadruples during the Vermont Maple Festival, but we'll tap into that later. Bwuah-ha-ha-ha-ha-ha! . . . Ah . . . um . . . ahem.

Sorry.

St. Albans has a history steeped in railroading, which began when it, with its close proximity to Lake Champlain, became a popular shipping route during the Industrial Revolution. St. Albans is now the northern terminus of the Vermonter, an all-coach train operated by Amtrak. The Vermonter (they should rename it "the Vermonner") operates daily from St. Albans City to and from Washington, D.C., and points between. The Vermonter used to continue from St. Albans City to Montreal, and it was then aptly called "the Montrealer."

In Barre-esque fashion, St. Albans Town—a separate municipality—surrounds St. Albans City. Some residents in both communities back a merger, and that could happen, once the city and town put to rest some long-standing political differences and the ships land from Mars.

Montpelier

Yes, it's still the smallest capital in the United States, with a population of only 8,000.

Yes, it's still the nation's only McDonald's-less capital.

And, yes, with Barre, they still form the "twin cities"—Vermont's very own version of Jagger and Richards.

And, heck, Montpelier and Portland, Maine, share the Valentine Phantom (or Valentine Bandit), an anonymous someone who plasters the downtown area with hearts every February 14.

But Montpelier is the only capital in America where it's best that your feet smell. Since the late 1970s, the city has also been known as the Rotten Sneaker Capitol of America, thanks to the International Rotten Sneaker Contest, sponsored by Odor-Eaters since 1988.

Young competitors ages five to fifteen and their healthy sweat glands first compete in regional contests, and those winners—who have ranged from Alaskans to Italians—bring their smelliest, dirtiest, most worn-out sneakers to Montpelier for the spring contest. The winner earns a $500 U.S. Savings Bond and a year's supply of Odor-Eaters. The winners' shoes then get a spot in the Hall of Fumes.

For anyone brave enough, they always need judges.

The Vermont Statehouse—where laws are made and law-makers snooze—is a Greek Revival structure and the third building on the same site to serve as the capitol building. It was designed in 1857, opened in 1859, and underwent a careful restoration project in the 1980s.

The building is on State Street, about a block north of the Winooski River, and is open Monday through Friday, with tours available every half-hour from July to October (so as not to wake the legislature, which is typically in session from January to May).

Winooski

Personally, I think it has the funniest-sounding name in the state. Its etymology comes from the Abenaki and means, "This is where the onions grow. I can tell by your breath."

With about 6,500 people, Winooski is basically a suburb of the Burlington-South Burlington area. In 1979, the city actually researched construction of a 200-foot-high dome over the entire city, to reduce winter heating costs. (Yeah, I know. But, hey, it was 1979.)

In recent years, Winooski installed a roundabout, to ease traffic flow, as part of a downtown redevelopment project. Unfortunately, everyone from Highgate thinks it's a NASCAR track.

Newport

Newport has a population of 5,000. Something cool: Between 1936 and 1953, Newport's International Club had the largest dance floor in New England, capable of holding 2,000 people. Various performers stopped to entertain there while en route to Boston from Montreal. They included: Louis

Armstrong, Cab Calloway, Rosemary Clooney, the Dorsey Brothers, Gene Krupa, Glenn Miller, and Louis Prima.

I wonder how many of them met Maggie Little, the Pipe-Smoking Fisherwoman. For most of her adult life, five-foot-tall Maggie Little sat perched on a barrel, fishing daily atop the Canadian Pacific railway bridge on Lake Memphremagog. She always wore the same ratty skirt with an apron over it and drank bottled beer—some of it illegal.

Ironically, Maggie Little wasn't camera-shy. Passengers getting off the trains would often take her picture. In exchange, she requested tobacco.

She died in 1934, at age ninety-one.

I wish I'd known her.

Vergennes

With only 2,800 people, Vergennes is one of America's smallest established cities.

City envy. Big time.

Our largest towns, in order, are . . .

Essex

My friend Jennifer jokes that the only good thing to come out of Swanton is the entrance ramp to Interstate 89.

"Sure," I tell her. "But at least I'm not from Essucks."

I kid, of course.

At about 19,000 people, Essex is Vermont's largest town. The village of Essex Junction was formed within the town in 1892. If you don't ask an Essex resident if he is from the town or junction, he will slash your tires when you're not looking. That's the Essex way.

To date, Essex plays host to an IBM plant, which surprisingly became the state's largest dwindling employer; by the time you turn the page, it could be gone. (Got layoffs?)

Colchester

Winooski was part of Colchester until 1922, when Winooski broke off and started thinking that a giant bubble might be a good idea.

With about 17,000 residents, Colchester is known for its luxurious lakeside homes, one of which is owned by Tom "The Coach" Brennan, former UVM men's basketball coach and ESPN analyst since 1995.

Bennington

Tucked in the southeast corner of Vermont, Bennington has a population of about 16,000, which probably would be greater if not for the Bennington Triangle.

Author and folklorist Joseph Citro—who likely hates being called the "Stephen King of Vermont," but we're gonna go for it anyway—first coined the phrase "Bennington Triangle" on public radio in the early 1990s, while discussing an area near Glastenbury Mountain where several people disappeared from 1920 to 1950—eight between 1945 and 1950. (Enter *Twilight Zone* theme.)

Bennington is also home to Bennington College, a nationally recognized and pricey liberal arts school that opened as a women's college in 1932 and went co-ed in 1969. Bennington College's strengths are performing and creative arts—Martha Graham and Norman Lear taught there—and students develop their own course of study with faculty. Very smart people attend Bennington College, such as my friend Michelle, a 1988 grad who entered her freshman year at age sixteen.

"When I was living in North Bennington in the mid-1980s," said Michelle, "it had a pizza shop/ice cream parlor which would bake a Tony's frozen pizza and deliver it to your door; a Mexican restaurant; a balloon shop; and a newsstand where Mrs. Percy—then in her eighties—sold newspapers and magazines. Mrs. Percy had an extensive collection of porn magazines, which she would offer to unsuspecting newspaper purchasers."

Admit it, you want to see Bennington now, don't you?

While you're there, you can brush up on Vermont history. In addition to its claim about the so-called Battle of Bennington in 1777, Bennington is one of the most historical areas of the state. It is the site of the first Vermont schoolhouse; the Catamount Tavern; the Green Mountain Boys' meeting room; and abolitionist William Lloyd Garrison's printing shop.

Brattleboro

One winter weekend, I went to Brattleboro—population 12,000—strolled through its charming and artistically bustling downtown, searched for a unique but local dining experience, and ended up on a barstool in a Ninety-Nine restaurant, at the edge of town.

Good thing I did; otherwise I might not have discovered the Strolling of the Heifers or "Super" Bill Kathan, which I did, thanks to my waitress, Jenn, a twenty-three-year-old "Bratt" native.

"It's huge," Jenn said of the heifer stroll (www.strollingofthe heifers.com). "This town is packed."

In 2001, a concerned group of town leaders and farmers organized the Strolling of the Heifers—a slower and safer version of Spain's Running of the Bulls—to make people more aware of Vermont's struggling family farms. The first and each subsequent stroll has been held on the first weekend in June, during National Dairy Month.

Children and heifers lead the parade, followed by farmers, cows, bulls, horses, goats, poultry, floats, tractors, bands, clowns, and more. According to Jenn, there is a "super poop cleanup team" that brings up the rear of the parade, wielding brooms and donning capes.

That would be an easy job for sinewy "Super" Bill Kathan, who might be Vermont's most physically fit dude. He holds more than forty world records and calls himself "The Exercise Champion of the World." Since 2000, he has frog-jumped ten meters in 6.4 seconds, completed 24,360 leg lifts in six hours, and finished 1,084 abdominal crunches in fifteen minutes. In 2006, he set the world record for the most single-finger push-ups: twenty.

"I get little butterflies when I start," he told the *Concord* (N.H.) *Monitor*, which covered that event. "There's a shock the first two or three."

Bill, I'd be happy with one.

Ordinances did not prohibit public nudity in Brattleboro until July 2007, when nudists took advantage of the situation by walking upstreet to get a coffee and strolling home with their sugar cubes showing. By a three-to-two margin, town selectmen passed an emergency rule temporarily "banning nudity on the main roads and within 250 feet of any school or place or place of worship," among other places. That December, the board made the ban permanent.

The nudity fine in Brattleboro is now one hundred dollars. Dare me?

Send me a hundred bucks. I'll do it.

Hartford

About 10,000 people live in Hartford, on the New Hampshire border.

Milton

Milton has about 10,000 people, too, and is known throughout Vermont as the official birthplace of the glottal stop.

"Mil'on."

Springfield

Practically no one but the 9,000 people who live in Springfield even cared about Springfield until 2007, when the town was chosen from thirteen other Springfields nationwide to be the site of *The Simpsons Movie* premiere. Hollywood flocked to Springfield.

One year later, a major blaze purposely set by an upstairs tenant destroyed the Ellis Block building, which housed the movie premiere.

D'oh!

Even our smallest towns are exceptionally big in their own ways. Just look . . .

Barton

It only has 3,000 people and only covers about forty-five miles of area in my beloved Northeast Kingdom, but the story behind its namesake is a keeper.

William Barton, who co-founded the town, was an officer in the Continental Army during the Revolutionary War and later served as adjutant general of the Rhode Island militia.

At age sixty-four, Barton was confined under house arrest, because he wouldn't pay a public fine, even though he could afford it. At seventy-seven, he was released at the request of the visiting Marquis de Lafayette, who paid the balance of the fine.

That's right, Bartoneers, your town is named for a cheapskate.

Brandon

In late January 2006, I attended a meeting in St. Albans City sponsored by the Vermont Arts Council, which was co-organizing a statewide art exhibit that would be the largest ever in the state: Palettes of Vermont. The VAC distributed 6,000 wooden artists' palettes throughout Vermont, for any use (fabric, sculpture, paint, photography), in any medium (poetry, film, theater, dance).

At our January organizational session, I met the smallest firecracker with the biggest bang I'd ever encountered up to that point in my life: Warren Kimble.

Warren is an internationally renowned folk artist who helped polish Brandon's cultural side in 2001, when he and a handful of other Brandon artists formed a guild with no money and no space. They persuaded a Brandon bank to let them display work in its empty building until they could pay for the space.

"None of us cared about money," Warren said. "And here we were, trying to make money."

To do that, they collected donations for manufactured fiber-glass pigs, got artists to paint them, and raised $180,000 through an auction, which paid for the bank building purchase and renovation. The Pigs of Brandon spawned the Birdhouses of Brandon and Brandon Rocks—a display of marvelously painted rocking chairs.

Brandon, population 4,000, went from being a pock on Vermont's face to one of the state's largest tourist attractions, with a great, locally owned downtown.

"You have to be creative and do your own show, whatever it is," Warren told those of us who listened to him in St. Albans.

So we did. For Palettes of Vermont, two dozen Franklin County residents constructed, built, and displayed the world's largest art palette, which featured a Vermont design by Franklin County artist Natalie Larocque Bouchard. The Vermont media jumped all over that palette, thanks to inspiration from Warren Kimble—our human Doors song.

He lit our fire.

Brookfield

The town, with about 1,300 people, boasts that it has the state's oldest, continually running library, dating back to 1791, but it has something else that has attracted thousands more.

There is a floating bridge on Sunset Lake, supported by floating barrels, because the lake is too deep for traditional pilings. The short, wooden span is the only floating bridge east of the Mississippi River, and was built in 1820 by Luther Adams and his neighbors.

Damage sometimes closes the floating bridge, but it is drivable, even though it has caused even the toughest Harley rider to turn back and seek a drier detour.

Cavendish

If I had to guess, Cavendish is the basis for this famous phrase: "I need that like I need a hole in the head."

Cavendish has 1,500 people and covers 400 square miles. Russian writer and Nobel Prize winner Aleksandr Solzhenitsyn

Just down Route 7 from Brandon you'll find the state's tallest resident: Queen Connie. She is a nineteen-foot-tall gorilla that holds up a golden Volkswagen Bug in front of Pioneer Auto Sales.

(This was a brilliant marketing scheme by the gang at Pioneer, because when motorists suddenly stop to gawk at Connie, and someone hits them from behind, they don't have to look far for a new car.)

lived in Cavendish after the Soviet Union exiled him in 1974, but even he might not be the man with the most incredible tie to the town.

That would be Phineas Gage.

On September 13, 1848, Gage was foreman of a work crew that blasted rock while clearing the roadbed for a new rail line outside Cavendish. After a hole was drilled into the body of the rock, Gage was responsible for adding gunpowder, a fuse, and sand, and then tamping the charge down with a large iron rod.

Unfortunately, at one point, he forgot the sand.

Around four-thirty that afternoon, he hit the fuse with the rod and the powder exploded. The rod—one and a quarter inches round, three feet, seven inches long, and thirteen and a quarter pounds—went through one side of Gage's face, shattered his jaw, shot through the back of his left eye, exited at the top of his head, and landed about eighty feet away.

I apologize if you're eating right now, but that's not even the best part. Don't take another bite yet.

Within minutes, Gage was walking with little or no help and sat upright for the three-quarter-mile ride to a doctor's office in town. Drs. Edward H. Williams and John Martyn Harlow noticed Gage was weak from hemorrhage, but he had a regular pulse of about sixty. He was alert and coherent—a walking, talking miracle.

Gage never fully recovered and sustained serious brain damage, although there is evidence that he capitalized on his near-fatal injury by making himself a sideshow spectacle in some areas of the Northeast. He held another job in New Hampshire and also lived in Chile for a period of his life. He died in 1860, around the age of thirty-seven.

Gage's friends said he was never the same after the accident, which can happen to a man when he becomes famous, and when a frickin' pole darts through his frickin' head.

Charlotte

Charlotte and other small Vermont towns face a common struggle—the constant mispronunciation of their names.

It's "Char-lot," not "Char-lit," as in North Carolina. Residents of and visitors to "callous"–spelled "Calais"—know just what I'm talking about.

My fondest memories of Charlotte are the Jerry Jeff "Mr. Bojangles" Walker shows I saw at the Old Lantern, sometime around 2004 and 2005. The Old Lantern—which features a maple-wood dance floor—is an 1800s-era barn that was renovated to accommodate 350 people for concerts, banquets, receptions, and lots of sweaty people who really enjoy hearing Jerry Jeff belt his classic song, "Up Against the Wall, You Redneck Mother"—not once but TWICE during the same show.

Seems fitting he sang that twice in Vermont.

Chester

Chester—population 3,000—is known for its stone village, a section of houses made of local granite along Route 103 that is a popular tourist attraction and is listed on the National Register of Historic Places.

From September 1886 to July 1902, a nighttime burglar conducted a string of fifty robberies in Chester. The perpetrator targeted homes, mills, farm supply stores, and other buildings. Town selectmen offered a $500 reward to whoever apprehended the criminal.

Then, one night, fed-up gristmill owner Charles H. Waterman booby-trapped a window in his business with a shotgun, which planted a bullet in the leg of the burglar during his next attempt.

The culprit?

Clarence Adams, one of the town selectmen, founder of the local library, incorporator of the Chester Savings Bank, and (enter "Hallelujah Chorus" here), a state lawmaker.

Rumors abound as to why Adams—dubbed "The Gentlemen Burglar"—took to fleecing his own community. Some say he had a lifelong love for adventure. Others say he had a dual personality. After all, a copy of Robert Louis Stevenson's *Strange Case of Dr. Jekyll and Mr. Hyde* was found on his bookshelves.

Adams was convicted and went to prison, where he either died or faked his death and fled to Canada in 1904.

This, of course, begs an obvious question: How did Charlie Waterman spend his reward money?

Derby Line

This tiny village—about 700 residents in just less than one square mile—sits on the Canadian border in the town of Derby.

Derby Line actually runs contiguously with the Rock Island district of Stanstead, Quebec. Derby Line and Stanstead share water and sewer systems and emergency crews, which respond to calls on both sides of the border.

In some spots, the border actually runs through homes, meaning meals made in one country are devoured in another. The border also divides a tool-and-die factory once operated by the Butterfield division of Litton Industries.

Concerned about illegal immigration, U.S. border officials have shown interest in closing some Derby Line streets that have historically run into those in Stanstead. In 2007, the Derby Line trustees met in joint session with the Stanstead Council and mayor—on Canadian soil, using Vermont procedural rules.

The Haskell Free Library and Opera House was built smack dab on the border in 1904, meaning it's in two countries. The library collection and the opera stage are in Stanstead, but the door and most opera seats are in Derby Line. Therefore, the Haskell is sometimes called the only library in the U.S. with no books and the only opera house in the U.S. with no stage.

Glover

Glover is best known as the home of Bread & Puppet, a politically radical giant-puppet theater company founded by director Peter Schumann in New York City, in the early 1960s. Schumann moved Bread & Puppet to Vermont in 1970.

Why "Bread & Puppet"? Because the troupe treats audiences to fresh bread and a garlic-based dipping sauce during each performance.

Bread & Puppet's best-known work was the Domestic Resurrection Circus, performed annually in the Big Apple and then Glover until 1998, when large crowds became unmanageable and—in one tragic instance—violent. Bread & Puppet still performs and participates in some protests.

Luckily, I can say I've performed with Bread & Puppet—in 1990, during an educational week studying improvisational acting with the Governor's Institute on the Arts. Bread & Puppet organizers chose students' roles based on their skills and talent.

I got to be a horse's ass.

After the performance, a professional actor told me I could be "the next Ernest Borgnine."

I still hold out hope.

Highgate ("Oygate")

Highgate only has 3,400 people, numerous dairy farms, and a major highway—Route 78—that runs along the Missisquoi River. Yet it probably has more in common with New York City than any other Vermont town, due to one factor and one factor only. It has boroughs: Highgate Center, Highgate Falls, Highgate Springs, and East Highgate. Some even have different zip codes. How ghetto is that?

Jamaica

No, mon, not dat Jamaica.

Kirby

What else can you say about a town that has less than 500 people and a set of six-foot jacks and a ball stuck in the middle of a field? Artist David Tanych sculpted the oversized toys and displayed them in a field owned by he and his wife, Meryl Lebowitz, also an artist.

Apparently, they couldn't get an Act 250 permit for a Rubik's Cube.

Manchester

First thing's first—I dig Manchester. If that sounds like a disclaimer, it is. You'll soon see why.

Manchester is a popular destination for out-of-staters from New York and Connecticut and offers a wide mix of local businesses and factory outlet stores by national chain retailers, such as Brooks Brothers and Ralph Lauren.

Robert Todd Lincoln, the only one of Abraham Lincoln's four sons to live past adolescence, owned a summer-home-turned-tourist-attraction in Manchester, called Hildene. Members of the alternative rock band The Samples are Manchester natives, and actor Treat Williams (*Hair, Things to Do in Denver When You're Dead*) has a home there.

But the reason I dig Manchester so much is because of the great Northshire Bookstore, though it was an acquired taste, admittedly. My first trip there occurred during ski season—passes on jacket zippers galore. I didn't have one—clearly a minority.

"Excuse me, sir," one of the café employees said, as I worked alone at a long, wooden table. "Would you mind moving to the back, to the Wi-Fi bar?"

"To the back?" I asked. Calm at first, until I thought more about it. "No! I WON'T move to the back! I'm staying here, and there ain't nothin' you can do about it!"

Right then, I was the Rosa Parks of bookstore cafés.

(Publisher's note: Actually, Leon informed us during a meeting about this book that he quietly packed his things and obliged the café worker, because he's a major wimp, and because his sandwich was awesome and he really wanted to finish it.)

Marlboro

In 2006, Marlboro, population 1,000, was one of the first American towns whose citizens passed a resolution that endorsed impeaching President George W. Bush.

Teeny-tiny liberal arts school Marlboro College, which gets high marks from academic publications, is—surprise!—in Marlboro. (Famous Marlboro dropouts include actor Ted Levine, Jame Gumb from *Silence of the Lambs*; and Chris "Mr. Big" Noth, from *Sex and the City*.) The late children's book author and illustrator Tasha Tudor also lived in Marlboro.

If you're ever in Marlboro, check out the Southern Vermont Natural History Museum. It's at the Hogback Mountain Scenic Overlook on Route 9, about thirteen miles west of Brattleboro and twenty-seven miles east of Bennington. This small museum is basically the life's work of Luman Ranger Nelson, a renowned New England taxidermist who collected the animals from 1900 to 1962. The odd collection has more than 650 taxidermy specimens in small dioramas, including a dozen albinos (groundhog, red squirrel, gray squirrel, robin, barn swallow, deer, porcupine, etc.). The museum also has a doe with horns and three extinct birds (passenger pigeon, heath hen, and Eskimo curlew).

There is also a display of non-releasable live hawks and owls. If one gets out, close your eyes. Or run.

Middlebury

Middlebury is home to prestigious Middlebury College, founded in 1800, and the prestigious Bread Loaf Writers' Conference, which I won't have to worry about paying for, because I write about fish named "Buster."

Remember that slick, pompous, BMW-driving germ who couldn't spell "the," but somehow graduated in the top 2 percent of your class, and you would have punched him, if only his daddy wasn't waiting on the sidelines with his team of lawyers, waiting to sue you?

The bad news: He went to Middlebury, and you didn't.

The good news: Someone has probably punched him by now.

Middlebury is so prestigious, you almost hate to mention Moo-Doo.

Almost.

Moo-Doo is a popular line of bagged cow, horse, and poultry compost sold as a partnership between Vermont Natural Ag Products and Foster Brothers dairy farm; they say Moo-Doo is "udderly the best."

Jeezum crow.

Morrisville

For years, I only thought of Morrisville as the midpoint to Lyndon State College from Swanton. Little did I know Morrisville has two country clubs, a hospital, and an airport.

I was in college. I really wasn't paying attention to anything in Morrisville except the Route 2 McDonald's.

In April 2005, Morrisville had a turn on the national map when seventeen-year-old Nicholas Buckalew took grave robbing to a new level. He broke into a tomb, removed a corpse's head with a hacksaw, and hid it near his apartment.

Why?

He planned to use the skull as a water bong.

"The widow was in shock," the Morrisville police chief said at the time. "She did not want any information. She did not want to know any details.

"He was a peculiar person, put it that way. He was peculiar."

Ya think?

Moscow

Have I been there? Nyet.

New Haven

New Haven is the home of Evergreen Cemetery, which is best known for the tomb of Timothy Clark Smith, whose 1893 crypt includes a window to help him escape, in case he was buried alive.

Mr. Smith, you can come out now.

Quechee/Woodstock

This is where I go in Vermont when I want quiet time in my head, or time with a dear friend.

After you gaze upon majestic Quechee Gorge—the state's version of the Grand Canyon—go have lunch at The Farmers Diner, a bus converted to an eatery, and then spend hours at the Quechee Gorge Village & Arts Center, where there is a glassblowing studio, an antique mall, and a winery.

In Woodstock, near Quechee on Route 4 West, it always feels like a bus of transplants has pulled into the center of town and exploded. Need a reminder you're in Vermont? Pull up to Woodstock Hardware and check out the marquee, which will often say something like, "If duct tape didn't fix it, you didn't use enough duct tape." (They must've got that one from Slim Bovat.)

Richmond

Richmond's Old Round Church—actually a sixteen-sided polygon—was built between 1812 and 1814 under the direction of local blacksmith and carpenter William Rhodes as a multidenominational place of worship for Baptists, Christians, Congregationalists, Methodists, and Universalists.

Why round? One legend said it was to keep the devil out of any corners.

Royalton

Most people know Royalton as the home of Vermont Law School. (Incidentally, Vermont is one of the few remaining states where residents can be lawyers without attending law school. They only have to read the law—which is unfortunate if you're illiterate—and pass the bar.)

Personally, I like Royalton for Oliver Plaistead.

It's the Civil War. Oliver Plaistead, of East Barnard, doesn't want to fight. In Grinch-like fashion, he leaves home and moves to a cave high on nearby Ellis Mountain, in Royalton. He spends the war hiding in "Oliver's Cave," as it's known today, later returns to East Barnard, and lives the rest of his life in a shack on Brook Road, until he dies at age fifty-eight, almost two decades after the war ends.

Sharon

Sharon native Jim Fisk sits behind the counter of the Sharon Trading Post—an auto body shop since the 1920s that he converted to a general store in 1985—and quickly spits out the name of the utmost authority on his hometown.

"Phyllis Potter," he says, as my eyes shift to the locked, glass case filled with firearm ammo. Jim's store serves lots of hunters, which is also evident by the city of beef jerky canisters at the checkout counter. The Sharon Trading Post is busiest from six until eight in the morning and from three in the afternoon until closing.

"People says, 'Put in a deli,' " Jim says, the day I visit his store. "I says, 'I'm not that hungry.' "

123

Out in my car, I dial Phyllis's number. With her thick Vermont accent—"they-ah" and "hee-yah" pepper her conversations—she tells me she's gotta make it quick, because she and her husband are goin' snowmobilin' in a few minutes.

She's in her mid-seventies.

Phyllis describes Charles Downer, one of Sharon's founders and a local philanthropist who left gobs of land and money for various causes. At one time, his name hung on a sign over every culvert that flowed through property he once owned.

Sharon was chartered in 1761, Phyllis says. How it got its feminine name is a mystery, though her best guess is it's because some of its first settlers were from Sharon, Connecticut.

 Asked for a good Sharon story, Phyllis Potter mentions the Old Home Days chicken pie dinner and church program that happened when she was a little girl. This particular year, the church floor suddenly dropped eight to ten inches, with everyone inside. The congregation scrambled for the doors and windows.

After everyone vacated safely, they simply continued their service on the front lawn, while Civilian Conservation Corps workers fixed the floor. But, what happened to it?

"I have no i-deer," Phyllis says. "It's always been fine evah since."

"That's the best I could evah find out about that," she says. "It's kind of a mystery, but we don't dwell on it."

10

Doin's

For years, I spent a week each summer at the Swanton Summer Festibal.

Yes, you read that right—"festibal." See, in Vermont, there are "festivals," where people with no-vacancy wallets fork out what I know as a mortgage payment to sit on posh blankets, drink good wine, eat strong cheese, and listen to classical music or jazz.

Then there are "festibals," where people with little money spend lots of it on lots they could live without, all packed into an area the size of a boxing ring. Festibals usually have themes, such as maple syrup or milk.

I first heard the term "festibal" from Aunt Ruthie, whose children, Eli and Sara, made her live at the festibal. Really. For the whole four days the festibal was in town, they spent their days and nights there, sometimes camping out in Scrambler buckets and surviving on fried dough.

"Ya takin' the kids to the festibal?" she'd ask my parents every summer, her eyes widening with excitement.

"Probably," my parents replied, "but we hate to."

"Why?"

"There's nothing for them at the festibal."

In retrospect, they were wrong. What about that festibal game where the yellow rubber duckies with numbers written on their tail feathers floated around a track of finger-numbing water? Once, I picked one of those ducks and won a plastic snake that, if I held it right, looked real to my dense, young brain.

In high school, cool kids avoided the festibal. We'd test each other out during summer vacation, the week before the festibal arrived, as we met on the village streets and verbally bashed the latest New Kids on the Block hit we all knew the words to.

"You goin' to the festibal this weekend?"

"Yeah . . . right. Like I'd go to the festibal." (Pregnant pause.) "Uh . . . you?"

"Shee-ya! Why would I do that?"

"I know. It's so lame."

"Strictly for losers."

Sure enough—we'd see each other at the festibal.

And never mention it again.

That's what a festibal is about: griping about it before it happens, telling everyone you hate it and won't go, and then running into everyone there who says they despise it as much as you. The reality is—they don't. How can they? It's a festibal!

Every festibal has a parade, too, featuring: at least one Shriners troupe in mini-cars, 12,000 fire and rescue vehicles, livestock, livestock poop-sweepers, anyone running for office (particularly during an election year), and at least a half-dozen people on floats that think it's fun to pelt candy at little children. My childhood home was on the festibal parade route, which annually garnered me tons of popularity with the other neighborhood kids—for a whole forty minutes.

I mainly attend festibals now to get an Italian sausage with cooked onions and peppers, and to people-watch, because, really, a festibal is only as good as its crowd. Looking for the latest trends in fishnet T-shirts and white Spandex? Eager for an innovative new way to scream profanities at your children from three football fields away? Curious as to how many women still use six cans of hair spray for a night out? Wondering if there are any Ratt, Warrant, or Twisted Sister fans left in the world?

A festibal is the place for you.

A popular fund-raiser at Vermont festibals is cow plop bingo, where someone with lots of time and chalk on his hands draws a grid decorated with 500 equally proportioned, numbered squares. Then, a cow roams the grid. If she plops on your number, you win prize money—typically around $500. If you're standing close enough to her when she plops, you win a trip to the shower to wash your shins.

Vermont festivals, festibals, and fairs

Spring

- Vermont Maple Festibal: St. Albans, April (www.vtmaple festival.org)
- Discover Jazz Festival: Burlington, spring (www.discover jazz.com)

Summer

- Festival of the Arts: Waitsfield, August (www.vermontart fest.com)
- Festival on the Green: Middlebury, July (www.festivalon thegreen.org)
- Champlain Valley Fair: Essex, August, (www.cvfair.com)
- Caledonia County Fair: Lyndonville, August (www.vtfair.com)
- Addison County Fair and Field Days: New Haven, August (www.addisoncountyfielddays.com)

- Franklin County Field Days: Highgate, late summer, (www.franklincountyfielddays.org.)
- Vermont State Fair: Rutland, summer (www.vermontstate fair.net)
- Vermont Dairy Festibal: Enosburg, June (www.vermont dairyfestival.com)
- Green Mountain Chew Chew Food and Music Fest: Burlington, June (www.greenmountainchewchew.com)
- Vermont Mozart Festival: various sites, July (www.vtmozart.com)

Fall

- Killington Brew Fest: Killington, September (www.killington.com)
- Vermont Apple Festival & Craft Show: Chester, Columbus Day Weekend (www.springfieldvt.com)
- Vermont Granite Festival—Barre (Where else?), September (www.granitemuseum.org)

Winter

- Stowe Winter Carnival: Stowe, January (www.stowewinter carnival.com)
- St. Albans Winter Carnival: St. Albans, February (www.st albansvt.com)
- Vermont Mozart Festival: various sites, December and January (www.vtmozart.com)

(Vermont has at least a dozen more annual music festivals scattered throughout the state. To learn more about them, or other festibals I might've missed here, inquire with the Vermont Chamber of Commerce at www.vtchamber.com.)

Indoor activities

If the weather is too icky for festibal-hopping—which should be an official Vermont sport—check out these other spots for fun, inexpensive, indoor activities:

American Museum of Fly Fishing

In Manchester, it features rods owned by Babe Ruth, Ernest Hemingway, and George W. Bush. (www.amff.com)

American Society of Dowsers Headquarters and Bookstore

Modern followers of "water witching"—the art of finding buried objects with a Y-shaped stick—can find guides and resources at this shop in Danville. Incidentally, Lyndon State College hosts the annual American Society of Dowsers Conference. (www.dowsers.org)

Bennington Museum

It focuses mainly on the Revolutionary War battle that didn't occur in town but gave Vermont state workers a day off every year. However, another room features works by Anna Mary Robertson "Grandma" Moses, who lived in Bennington from 1927 to 1935. (www.benningtonmuseum.org)

Billings Farm & Museum

The estate of Frederick Billings, a Woodstock native who had a successful law career in San Francisco during the Gold Rush and returned home in 1870 to save his struggling hometown. (www.billingsfarm.org)

Cold Hollow Cider Mill

Sure, the cider's great, but what you really want is one of those awesome doughnuts from this gem tucked in Waterbury Center. (www.coldhollow.com)

ECHO Lake Aquarium and Science Center

Near Burlington's waterfront, this hands-on experience offers tons of displays about the lake and its geology, and theme exhibits about dinosaurs and human bodily functions have added some welcome diversity. (www.echovermont.org)

Estey Organ Museum

This celebrates the Estey Organ Company, which once produced more than a half-million organs and employed more than 500 people in Brattleboro. (www.esteyorganmuseum.org)

Eureka Schoolhouse

Vermont's oldest one-room schoolhouse, in Springfield. (www.historicvermont.org/sites/html/eureka.html)

Fairbanks Museum and Planetarium

This natural history museum—actually a Victorian exhibition hall—in St. Johnsbury features parrots, polar bears, an Egyptian mummy, and Japanese fans. The museum is also home to the Vermont Public Radio weather program, *Eye on the Sky*. (www.fairbanksmuseum.org)

Mary Meyer Museum of Stuffed Toys

In Townshend, you can watch how they're made and buy a new one. (www.bigblackbear.com)

Missisquoi National Wildlife Refuge

Granted, this one is still outside, with miles of walking trails on hundreds of acres of preserved federal land in Swanton, but you can always wait for the rain to let up in the refuge head-quarters, which houses displays about the national refuge system and what critters you'll see along the Missisquoi River. (www.fws.gov)

Morgan Horse Farm, University of Vermont (Burlington)

The Morgan breed has long been linked with Vermont. Videos and tours happen every hour. (www.uvm.edu/morgan)

New England Maple Museum

Right there in Pittsford. (www.maplemuseum.com)

New England Transportation Institute and Museum

It makes sense that White River Junction—probably, along with St. Albans, the hub of state railroad history—would contain this tribute to the state's once-thriving reliance on tracks. (www.newenglandtransportationmuseum.org)

Norman Rockwell Museum of Vermont

Just off Route 7 in Rutland, the Norman Rockwell Museum doesn't contain any of his original works, but it does showcase his illustrious career, part of which he spent in southern Vermont. (www.normanrockwellvt.com)

Porter Music Box Museum

Just like the Estey Organ Museum, only this one's in Randolph, and it's dedicated to the Porter Music Box company, which still makes them on-site. (www.portermusicbox.com)

St. Albans Historical Museum

St. Albans plays hosts to Civil War relics and a room dedicated to Sterling Weed, a local music instructor who, at the age of one hundred, was once the nation's oldest active bandleader. There is also a model of Phineas Gage's head (remember the iron rod through it?), and another display about a man who had a flap over his stomach so he could oversee his digestive process. (Seriously . . .) (www.stamuseum.com)

Shelburne Museum

Probably the most popular site for school field trips in the state—can't tell you how many times I went there before high school—the Shelburne Museum has thirty-eight buildings displaying thousands of Americana items, including a full-size steamship and horse-drawn vehicles. (www.shelburnemuseum.org)

Vermont Folklife Center

Basically, this is Middlebury's perfect homage to true Vermont rednecks. Expect to hear and see lots of words and phrases you learned earlier in the book. (www.vermontfolklife center.org)

Vermont Ski Museum

In Stowe's former town hall, there is a plasma screen with ski videos, several exhibits, and a Hall of Fame featuring pivotal figures in state ski history. (www.vermontskimuseum.org)

Vermont Teddy Bear Company

The flagship store and factory of probably the most famous teddy bear in the world is on Route 7 in Shelburne. See how they're made and buy one, too. (www.vermonttcddybear.com)

Vermont Toy & Train Museum

Geeks take note—they DO have action figures from *Star Trek, Star Wars*, and *Lost in Space*. Beam yourself to Quechee! Now! (www.quecheegorge.com/vermont-toy-train.php)

(Did I mention Vermont has museums?)

Nightlife

When he was in high school, my friend, Eric, used to hang out at the Steinhour Café, in Highgate. The Steinhour had a pool table and a jukebox that played both "Aqualung" and "Freebird." The cook never changed the french fry grease, "so they were incredibly tasty," Eric recalls.

Shortly after a management change, the Steinhour clientele also changed—to a more, shall we say, "authentic" Highgate crowd. One night, Eric was playing pool at Steinhour when a fight broke out. Just as Eric made way for the back door, Rosie, the manager, yelled, "Okay! Pick up the ketchups! It's time to close!"

"I just loved that line," Eric says today. "That's what nightlife in Vermont is all about."

Well, a good part of it anyway. True, there is a certain population in Vermont that spends its nights glued to television, or drinking beer around backyard bonfires, or tipping cows. But performing arts also abound in Vermont. Where can you catch a show?

The Flynn Center for the Performing Arts

Probably the cultural hub of Burlington and Vermont. I have seen Johnny Cash, Willie Nelson, Jethro Tull, a Pink Floyd tribute band, off-Broadway versions of *Rent* and *Cabaret*, and local

productions of *Grease* and *A Christmas Carol*, all at the Flynn
(www.flynncenter.org). Burlington also has Nectar's (where
Phish built its phan base) and Club Metronome.

Higher Ground

It opened in Winooski. Then it moved to South Burlington,
and has become the state's premier music venue for diverse
national acts (The Black Crowes, Wu-Tang Clan, and Judy
Collins) and popular Vermont musicians (The Nobby Reed
Project, Gregory Douglass, and the Starline Rhythm Boys).
(www.highergroundmusic.com)

Vergennes Opera House

My first show here was a 2008 solo performance by Byrds
co-founder Roger McGuinn. I was arm's length from greatness.
What a great, intimate venue. (www.vergennesoperahouse.org)

Paramount Theatre

Over decades, Rutland's nineteenth-century hall has drawn
such big-name performers as Harry Houdini, Groucho Marx,
and Branford Marsalis. (www.paramountvt.org)

Latchis Theatre / Hooker-Dunham Theater & Gallery

Both in Brattleboro, the historic Latchis—which doubles as
a hotel—shows contemporary films in a 750-seat theater decorated with Greek scenes. The Hooker-Dunham, on the other
hand, is all about avant-garde theater and performance art.
(www.latchis.com and www.hookerdunham.org)

Middlebury College Center for the Arts

It houses an intimate black-box theater, an artists' studio,
and a recital hall. (www.middlebury.edu/arts)

Barre Opera House

Features local productions and national performers, such as Woodstock '69 alum Richie Havens. (www.barreoperahouse.org)

Chandler Center for the Arts

This Randolph hall is the site of numerous plays and musicals, as well as the Central Vermont Music Festival in August and the Mud Season Variety Show in March. (www.chandler-center.org)

Middle Earth Music Hall

Inconspicuously hidden in Bradford, Middle Earth's acts play Irish tunes and belly dance. As for the real entertainers— they're on the barstools. (www.middle-earth-music.com)

Opera House at Enosburg Falls

Franklin County's hidden performing arts gem, which hosts the annual Vermont Dairy Festibal Pageant. (www.enosburg operahouse.org)

11

Jeet Yet?

My cousin Chris—affectionately known to me as "Cuzzint Chris"—is a great cook. He fluently talks about seasonings, cooking temperatures, taste, and aroma, and once spent five hours cooking me the best Chinese dinner I ever had—far and above anything in Canada. Cuzzint Chris is well versed in Vermont's three basic food groups: moo, sweet, and brew.

Moo

Believe it or not, some Vermonters don't drink milk.

"Not me," Uncle Turk says. "I've seen where that shit comes from."

That would be a cow.

Contrary to popular belief, Vermont—even though it once had more cows than people—is not among the top four dairy states. Those are: California, Wisconsin, New York, and Idaho. Vermont is home to 150,000 cows that generate millions of pounds of milk and a helluva lotta bowls of Cheerios.

Vermont is known for its family farms, which are struggling and dying off, but I still believe there is a sliver of romance left in the state's dairy industry. Farming is still a community as well as an industry—despite a recent shift to technology that even Scotty couldn't handle. ("If you don't stop pullin' 'er teats like that, captain, she's gonna blow!")

Fun Fact

Vermonters use only three spices:
salt
pepper
ketchup

I never fully appreciated cows until my daughter arrived and thought they were milk-giving gods.

"Look, Daddy!" she exclaims in the car. "Cows!"

She's twenty-eight.

Kidding. She's six.

Now, thanks to her, I slow down if I pass a herd of cows grazing near the road, whether I'm running, walking, or driving. Cows talk with their eyes. Anyone that has seen a cow up close knows what I mean.

"What are you staring at?" cows say. "I ain't a zebra, ya know."

To many, a cow is a symbol of Vermont. Vermont artist Woody Jackson has most famously depicted the Vermont cow in his paintings and works that appear on Ben & Jerry's packaging and marketing displays.

During the 1980s, my friend Liz owned a kiosk on Church Street in Burlington that sold nothing but cow-related merchandise. T-shirts. Sweatshirts. Hats. Key chains. She dressed like a cow, too, until too many single guys asked if they could feel her udder. She was known as "The Cow Lady."

To some Vermont residents, though, a cow is more than just a state symbol. My friend Emily comes to mind. She comes from a line of Orwell dairy farmers.

"Every evening," Emily recalled, "Doug (a family friend that helped on the farm) and his brothers and sister had to round up the cows to bring them to the barn, to be milked. One of Doug's brothers decided he would try to ride one of the cows.

So he jumped right on, and the cow bucked him off. He landed face down in a pile of cow shit. I was told that is why no one rides cows."

According to Emily, Doug's father, Fred, never spoke. Not at dinner. Not in the barn. Never.

One afternoon, Fred was milking in his barn and dealing with a stubborn cow that wouldn't give any milk. The more Fred tried, the angrier she got. She even kicked Fred. He never said a word. Silence.

After the second kick, however, Fred stood up and walked around to the front of his cows. He picked up a shovel—a big one, with a square head—swung his hardest, and whacked the cow in the head.

"There," Fred muttered. "Now you'll milk."

He returned the shovel to its spot and went back to the stunned cow.

She milked.

When Emily was little, her family had only three cows named Peter, Paul, and Harry.

That's right . . . Peter. Paul. And Harry.

Emily was an adult before she learned that those were the three names rotated among numerous cows that her family slaughtered for beef.

As long as Vermont makes Ben & Jerry's, we'll have dairy farms. And weight gain.

In 1977, Ben Cohen and Jerry Greenfield decided, "Hey, let's take this five-dollar correspondence course on ice cream from Penn State. Then, next year, we'll sell ice cream out of a renovated gas station in downtown Burlington."

This is when everybody realized they were hippies. Smart ones, too.

A man owned a small farm in Vermont. The labor department claimed he wasn't paying proper wages to his help and sent an agent out to interview him.

"I need a list of your employees and how much you pay them," the agent demanded.

"Welp," replied the farmer, "there's my farmhand, who's been with me for three years. I pay him two hundred a week, plus free room and board. The cook has been here for eighteen months, and I pay her one hundred fifty per week, plus free room and board. Then there's the half-wit who works about eighteen hours every day and does about ninety percent of all the work around here. He makes about ten dollars per week, pays his own room and board, and I buy him a bottle of whiskey every Saturday night. He also sleeps with my wife, occasionally."

"That's the guy I need to see," the agent said. "Where can I find him?"

"You're talkin' to 'im."

In 1979, they held their inaugural Free Cone Day—now an annual event nationwide—and combined their famous ice cream with a three-part mission statement that considered profits only one measure of success. The others were Product Mission (which generated profits), Economic Mission (which generated profits), and Social Mission (which generated profits).

In 1980, Ben and Jerry rented space in an old spool and bobbin mill in Burlington and started packing their product in its most famous incarnation: the pint. The following year, the first Ben & Jerry's franchise opened on Route 7, in Shelburne. And in 1983, Ben & Jerry's was used to build the world's largest ice cream sundae, in St. Albans. The sundae weighed 27,102 pounds. I had some, my first taste of Ben & Jerry's. I'll never turn back.

Breyers—pfffffft!

Ben & Jerry's is found in thirty global locations, from Aruba and Cyprus to Lebanon and Turkey. Every flavor is invented at the company headquarters, in South Burlington, by a four-man team of cool and creative ice cream geniuses known as "The Flavor Gurus." Discarded concoctions go to rest in the "Flavor Graveyard." The deceased include:

- American Pie: apple pie ice cream and apples and pie crust pieces
- Blondies Are a Swirl's Best Friend: chocolate low-fat ice cream packed with chunks of blond brownies and a fudge swirl
- Bovinity Divinity: chocolate ice cream and white fudge cows swirled with white chocolate ice cream and dark fudge cows
- Cool Britannia: vanilla ice cream with strawberries and fudge-covered shortbread
- Marsha Marsha Marshmallow: chocolate ice cream with fudge chunks and toasted marshmallow and graham cracker swirls (What? No Cindy Sorbet?)
- Oh Pear: pear ice cream with a hint of almond and a light fudge swirl
- Eggnog: Need I say more?
- And, my personal favorite, Chips 'n' Dip: sour cream 'n' onion ice cream with potato chips.
  Even genius is flawed, my friends.

In April 2000, Ben & Jerry's sold out to multinational food giant Unilever—the hippie thing to do. The ice cream makers celebrated their thirtieth anniversary in 2008 with a giant concert and party in Burlington, which I attended. I won tickets. Plus free samples. Tell me you wouldn't go.

The Ben & Jerry's manufacturing plant in Waterbury offers thirty-minute tours.

By the way, any coffee-lover will tell you the Ben & Jerry's of java is Green Mountain Coffee Roasters. Wild Mountain Blueberry. Yeeeaaahhh. (Starbucks, Schmarmucks. Pffft!)

We can't discuss Vermont Moo without a mention of Vermont cheese, and, by that, I mean Cabot.

The Cabot Creamery started in 1919, when ninety-four dairy farmers invested $3,700 into a dairy marketing cooperative. The group started by making butter with excess milk they produced, and moved on to cheese in 1930. In 2007, Cabot started marketing cheese internationally.

Cabot ain't the only fromage in town. The Vermont Cheese Council developed a Cheese Trail that includes thirty-nine cheese-makers in all corners of the state. Need a map? Visit www.vtcheese.com/cheesetrail.htm.

Sweet

We return now to our friend Kathy, who, you might recall, got terribly lost en route to a Fairfield sugarhouse.

"The first sugarhouse we visited was run the old-fashioned way, with horses hauling sap and wood for the fire that cooked it. It was a real treat to be offered warm syrup to drink.

"We then visited another sugarhouse, where we were offered maple sugar candy and had the opportunity to see an operation that used reverse osmosis to bring the sap to the sugarhouse. They still used wood for the fire.

"After that, we went to another sugarhouse, where the operation was totally modern, with reverse osmosis, and the sap was cooked by oil.

"It was a wonderful day, and we had a great time."

So many Vermont sugar-makers—with large and small operations—implement so many sugar-making methods, it's hard to follow all of them, or keep track of who's doing what. Today, though, I am going to reveal each and every sugar-maker's secrets, which start with one gal.

Aunt Jemima.

After the sugar-maker spends lots of time pretending he's tapping trees and boiling—to wow the money-spending tourists—he pours Aunt Jemima into big tin cans with pictures of horses and trees on them and sells each can for $499.95. Plus frickin' tax.

And that is how maple syrup is made.

"I don't believe you," you say. "If that's true about Aunt Jemima, then what about all those grades of syrup? Grade A Light

The New England Culinary Institute—regarded as one of the best culinary universities in the country—opened in Montpelier in June 1980 under Fran Voigt and John Dranow. Chef Michel LeBorgne—who has one of the best chef names EVER—taught the first class of seven students. A second campus opened in Essex in 1989, under the direction of a mustached chef who looked like a puppet with human hands and ended every sentence with "Bork, bork, bork!"

At NECI, students learn by doing. Employer demand for graduates is strong. Notable alumni include: Food Network staple Alton Brown; Steve Corry, owner and operator of Portland, Maine's Five Fifty-Five and one of *Food & Wine* Magazine's ten Best New Chefs of 2007; celebrity butler Paul Hogan; Steve Jackson, personal chef to the Chicago Bulls; and New York City chef Gavin Kaysen, once a contestant on *Next Iron Chef*.

NECI's student-to-chef ratio is small, and classes are conducted in real-kitchen situations. Courses include: Easy Bake Oven 101, The Art of The Pop Tart, and Why Mac & Cheese Matters in a Post-9/11 World.

Amber, Grade A Medium Amber, Grade A Dark Amber, Grade B. How do you explain that, Le-urn?"

That's easy.

I don't.

Some Vermonners will put syrup on anything, including snow. This is called "sugar on snow." If you're from out of state, and want to try this when you're here, I'll give you one tip for ensuring a perfect, tasty helping of sugar on snow: make absolutely sure the snow is yellow.

Each year, numerous sugarhouses across Vermont open to the public so that everyone can watch this fascinating process. Interested? Go to www.vermontmaple.org.

Brew

Lots of Vermonters are experts in light: Coors Light, Miller Lite, Michelob Light. There is also a huge sect of beer-drinkers that appreciates the fine beers made right in their backyard.

Breweries and brewpubs

Magic Hat Brewing Company, South Burlington
Otter Creek Brewing Company, Middlebury
Three Needs Taproom, Burlington
Vermont Pub & Brewery, Burlington
Rock Art Brewery, Morrisville
The Shed, Stowe
Kross Brewing Company, Morrisville
Gallagher's, Waitsfield
Trout River Brewing Company, East Burke
Harpoon Brewery, Windsor
Long Trail Brewing Company, Bridgewater Corners

Jasper Murdock's Alehouse, Norwich
Tunbridge Quality Ales, South Royalton
Black River Brewing Company, Ludlow
McNeill's Brewery, Brattleboro
Bennington Brewers Ltd., Bennington
Madison Brewing Company, Bennington
Windham Brewery, Brattleboro
Maple Leaf Malt & Brewing, Wilmington

(And so we don't upset the winos . . .)

Wineries and vineyards

Boyden Valley Winery, Cambridge
Snow Farm Vineyard & Winery, South Hero
Flag Hill Farm, Vershire (hard cider)
L'Abeille Honey Winery, Stowe
Grand View Winery, East Calais
Joseph Cerniglia Winery, Proctorsville
North River Winery, Jacksonville
Putney Mountain Winery, Putney

Real, other food

"Sure," you think. "I can get my share of milk, syrup, and good beer in Vermont. But what if I actually want to eat? Can you show me some good restaurants without telling me another story about a diner?"

Certainly.

A popular eatery among Lyndon State College students is the Miss Lyndonville Diner, which straddles Route 5, as you head toward St. Johnsbury from campus. Whenever I hit the Northeast Kingdom, I hit Miss Lyndonville. Sure, she hits back about two hours later, but she's worth it, man. Worth it.

In college, my friends and I would sometimes fill three tables at Miss Lyndonville, especially on all-you-can-eat-chicken night. For $5.99—it might've even been $3.99 now that I think about it—customers got all the fried chicken and sides they could devour. No limit on time or food.

I dug all-you-can-eat-chicken night. So did Tony, my roommate. Tony started lifting weights at age twelve and had a full, flowing mane of fiery red hair in college. He was big and friendly and sparked fear in the waitresses when he walked into the Miss Lyndonville Diner on all-you-can-eat-chicken night. We could hear them whispering in the kitchen: "We lose this time."

Tony's lifelong friend Chuck came to visit us at Lyndon State one weekend.

Fiddleheads

Vermont definitely has its share of homegrown and standout dishes. Gravy fries at Nectar's. Ben & Jerry's, of course. Anything with syrup on it. (Some Vermonters would eat this page if it had syrup on it.)

And then there are fiddleheads.

Fiddleheads are ferns that grow in soily sand along riversides. Harvested in the spring—early May is best, just as they are poking from the ground—fiddleheads are cooked like any other green, but they must be picked before they start unfurling. Cleaning them is tough, because they have a thin cover that must come off, and you have to rinse the sand from their furls—like when you go to the beach and sand gets in your furls.

Just a word of caution: Some varieties of fiddleheads contain carcinogens and have been linked to food poisoning. But don't worry—they taste just like chicken. Doesn't everything?

Naturally, we took him to all-you-can-eat-chicken night. Only Chuck didn't want chicken.

"Chuck," Tony said. "All the chicken you can eat, for that price, and you don't want it?"

"Nah," Chuck said. "Chuck's not hungry for chicken."

Our waitress arrived at our table.

"Hey, guys. What'll you have?"

"Chicken," Tony said.

"Chicken," I said.

Then, right there, at the Miss Lyndonville Diner, Chuck and our waitress engaged in what will forever go down as the best waitress-customer exchange in American history.

Chuck: "Waddaya got that's cheap?"

Waitress: "Probably you."

She didn't hesitate. She didn't pause. She didn't even stop writing.

This was before the days of "LOL" on the Internet, but believe me, Tony and I LOL-ed pretty frickin' hard at that.

As for other restaurants, well, there are just too many fine ones to list here. Check out www.hungryvt.com.

147

12

Where to Stay and Where to Spend Your Money

You can always find a place to stay in Vermont. Depending on where you stay, per-night prices will be higher by say, oh, approximately $10,000 during peak foliage and ski seasons.

My advice: Come in late August, or early September, when the weather's still hot, but lodging prices are still fair and reasonable. If you can't find a room at a hotel or motel, there are ample amounts of rural bed-and-breakfasts and inns, which are pricier than "outts."

Vermont is famous for its inns, mainly because they are not hotels, which look like, well, hotels. Our inns and bed-and-breakfasts look like old, mysterious, haunted homes, because, well, they are old, mysterious, haunted homes. Granted, inns do not offer the amenities or conveniences of a commercial establishment such as, oh, one that might rhyme with "Crawliday Spin." The Crawliday Spin has cable TV, free continental breakfast, and wireless Internet service. A Vermont inn has Bob Newhart. Camping is always an option. Stay at Maple Glen. Pack light.

Shopping

Vermont isn't just the land of Ben & Jerry's and Vermont Teddy Bears. Let's not forget Ethan Allen Furniture,

My farming friend Emily's grandmother, Patricia, was born in New York City, made her first trip to Vermont at three months old, and has lived in Fair Haven most of her life. (That's right: She's a transplant. You're catching on.)

Patricia's parents, Helen and Leo, and Emily's great-great-aunt Margaret headed north from the concrete jungle in Margaret's new car, the kind that had a bench as a backseat. As they came over the mountains in southern Vermont—Molly Stark Trail, I bet—they got stuck in the mud. Do you know what season it was? Wow, you really are paying attention.

Anyway, Leo noticed a farmhouse with the lights on, so he walked up to it.

Knock, knock, knock.

The farmer answered.

"You can stay here," he said upon hearing their plight. "Come on in."

"When they got to the farmhouse," Emily recalled, "the farmer and his wife got out of their warm bed and let them all sleep in their bed for the night."

Hammerhead Sleds, and Vermont Soapworks, just to name a few. And, of course, Bag Balm.

In 1899, Lyndonville resident John L. Norris bought the Bag Balm formula from its original creator in Wells River. Originally, Bag Balm was used as a salve to soften cow udders. Now, it boasts hundreds of uses, from soothing cracked and dry feet and hands to remedying sunburn and bicycle seat rash.

Bag Balm comes in a square, green tin with red lettering and a red clover, all surrounding a cow's head—very unique.

And, in fact, shopping in Vermont is unique itself. Amid the hordes of artisans' shops, art galleries, farmers markets, and souvenir shops lies an intriguing and aforementioned debate: big-box versus downtown. "Wal-Mart" is a dirty word for some folks in Vermont. The store is here, and more are proposed. Yet there is a sect of Wal-Mart-and-big-box haters in this state who are afraid such stores will kill our downtowns. I say, "Can't we all just get along? Frickers!"

Vermont's niche-oriented downtowns, especially Burlington's Church Street, sometimes field criticism for being too expensive, or geared toward tourists. Maybe you're not up to paying forty bucks for a candleholder, or three hundred for a frying pan. You have other options—Vermont redneck options, and no, not just the yard sale.

Some local radio programs air weekend-morning flea markets, where listeners call the host and describe an item they have, how much they want for it, and how a potential buyer can contact them.

Riiing . . . ring . . .

"Yee-ellow, welcome to the Tradin' Post. Waddaya got?"

"Mornin', Don. I'm sellin' my weed whacker."

"Okay, caller. How much do ya want for it?"

"Forty-five bucks. It's in good shape. Whacks my weeds real good, it does."

"And you say it's in good shape?"

"Yut."

"And you want forty-five dollars for it?"

"Yut."

"That sounds like a steal."

"I know. I can't throw my wife in air, too, can I?"

Craft shows

Craft shows are also popular in Vermont. A secret: I dig craft shows, or "reverse zoos," as I call them. I dig their culture, atmosphere—everything about them. Where else can you spend an entire weekend afternoon strolling around a church hall or school gym and buy a sequined pinecone, a stained-glass unicorn, or a ridiculous amount of sweatshirts with oversized busts of wolves, deer, and eagles plastered all over the front? Is there anywhere else you can eat homemade chili, corn chowder, and goulash, and then wash it all down with untold amounts of brownies and cookies topped with Hershey Kisses? All for less than ten bucks? And then, while you're enjoying yourself and checking out the homemade—and, in some cases, not-so-homemade—wares, you look up and realize the vendors are watching you. With a *Children of the Corn* kinda gaze.

Reverse zoos.

I say feed the animals.

Craft shows are homes of impulsive buyers. I once did a book signing at a holiday craft show. My friends and even some fellow authors laughed at the idea, until I told them I paid twenty dollars for my spot and sold twenty-two books in about five hours.

So if you see me at a craft show, stop by. Say "hi." And bring a brownie. I promise I won't get any crumbs on the book you buy.

Moms and Pops

Vermont is also known for its Moms and Pops—stores, that is. Mom and Pop stores are our little guys—the very businesses the militant anti-Wal-Marteers are trying to save. Mom and Pop stores offer more than a typical gas-and-potty station (especially in the way of personality) but less than a big-box store (except in the way of personality). If you're passing through, flatlanders, you can typically gas up, get an I HEART VERMONT T-shirt, take your pick of syrup and cheese, and pour yourself a Green Mountain Coffee, all while learning the store owner's first name and family history.

Perhaps the state's most famous general store is the Vermont Country Store (www.vermontcountrystore.com). Back when Pat Leahy was around 146 years old, country stores served as the supply points for people who couldn't travel their roads due to bad weather. Then, as Vermont grew and expanded, country stores fell by the wayside—until Vrest Orton restored the Vermont Country Store on Weston Common, in 1946. Today, the Vermont Country Store "is a Vermont vision of a country mall," as one tour guide put it, "with wood floorboards and rafters going back as long as a football field, and shelves packed with state-made products." The Vermont Country Store even has a catalog. Ironically, the Vermont Country Store is the Wal-Mart of Mom and Pops.

Galleries and specialty shops

Like Slim Bovat—remember him?—I could fill a trilogy of books on the hundreds of art galleries and specialty shops that pepper every nook, cranny, and crack of lovely, green Vermont. And there are dozens more ways to learn about each of them, either by calling each town's chamber of commerce, surfing the Internet, or just plain asking around.

But here's what I suggest.

Come to Vermont, look around for yourself. Find Vermont people, places, attractions, activities, food, and shops you love.

And just dig it.

13

That'll Learn Ya

This is the part of the book where you notice there are only a few pages left, and your insides feel that overwhelming sense of accomplishment.

But before I go, you impressed me so much with your knowledge of mud season and transplants in the last chapter, I thought I'd wrap things up with a little quiz. Don't worry—it's not hard. And I'll never know your score. One caveat: Be sure to check your answers on the next page before proceeding to the next question. Thanks. Here goes:

Questions

1. What does Slim Bovat claim he started doin' at age six?
   a) huntin'
   b) fishin'
   c) chewin' tabacka

2. "Coontuv" is . . .
   a) the main character in Alex Haley's *Roots*.
   b) a failed Ben & Jerry's flavor that included rice.
   c) a Vermonter's way of sayin' "could not have."

3. Which major rock act played two consecutive summer concerts in Oygate during the mid-1990s?
   a) The Who
   b) Pink Floyd
   c) Leon keeps forgetting

4. Which of these famous people isn't affiliated with Vermont?
   a) Rudyard Kipling
   b) David Mamet
   c) John LeClair

5. The best time to drive on Smugglers' Notch Road is . . .
   a) never
   b) see "a"
   c) at home, on YouTube

6. Pauline has worked at Rutland's Midway Diner since . . .
   a) seven o'clock this morning.
   b) Pat Leahy was elected to the U.S. Senate, sometime between 8500 and 7000 BC.
   c) Man, one mention of Midway, and I'm starvin'.

10. True or false? I'm not wearin' underwear right now.

Answers

1. The answer, according to this book, is "c," but it might be "a" and "b," too, for all I know. Never thought to ask him.
2. c
3. You said "c" didn't you? It was The Grateful Dead. Ha-ha! I remembered this time!

4. Actually, they all have ties to Vermont. Rudyard Kipling wrote *Captains Courageous* and *The Jungle Book* at his Brattleboro home. Totally overlooked him earlier. My bad.
5. Please don't come here and attempt it. Okay?
6. Seriously, I'm starving right now. How about we go back and skip up to the last question, so I can hit Midway?
10. Wouldn't you like to know? Or maybe not.

About the Author

Leon Thompson was born and raised in northwestern Vermont. A graduate of Lyndon State College, he is a staff reporter for the St. Albans, Vermont, *Messenger*, where he also writes a humor column. His humor writing has garnered him awards from the New England Press Association and the National Newspaper Association, among others. He is the author of two previous books, *Good Junk* and *dork: another look at my junk*.

Leon lives in St. Albans with his daughter.